The Sound of Many Waters

A Preacher's Potpourri

by Keith E. Knauss

Order From
MANNA MINISTRIES
8944 Westwind Dr.
Zeeland, MI 49464

© 1993 by Manna Ministries

All Rights Reserved

Printed by Newburgh Bible Publishers

DEDICATED

to

those dear people

under my ministry

who

in listening to the

sound of many waters

hear

the same things I do

CONTENTS

Chapter		Page
1.	Happiness	3
2.	When The Journey Is Too Great	7
3.	The Sound Of Many Waters	11
4.	Lonely Roads	13
5.	"Oh That I Were As...."	15
6.	Beyond The Visible	19
7.	"He Restoreth My Soul"	21
8.	Ministering	23
9.	Coming Home	25
10.	God's Finest Hour	29
11.	The Depths Of His Love	33
12.	The Mystery Of Godliness	37
13.	Altogether Lovely	39
14.	Where Flowers Never Fade	43
15.	Climbing Up The Rough Side	47
16.	My Lord And My God!	51

17. Amen And Amen!	55
18. "Abide With Me"	59
19. Dead...Yet!	61
20. Loneliness	65
21. The Consolations Of God	69
22. His Statutes My Songs	73
23. Just For The Record	77
24. "Now...But...Then"	81
25. No More!	85
26. Beyond The Tides Of Time	89
27. Eternity	91
28. Windswept	93

FOREWORD

It seems improbable that any other phrase could so well express the feeling of my heart as the words of the Apocalyptic Seer, who upon hearing our glorified Lord speak, said, "His voice was as the sound of many waters".

What a forceful figure and statement John gave. The words seem to be a reverberation of Psalm 29:3 in which we read, "The voice of Jehovah is upon the waters". The Psalmist had heard the musical voice of many waters and became lost in worship while extolling its might and majesty. Ezekiel also heard it and said, "His voice was like the sound of many waters" (Ezek. 43:2). And in the hearing of that voice Ezekiel saw the glory of God and it put him prostrate upon his face. John on lonely Patmos isle had the same experience and wrote, "His voice was as the sound of many waters" (Rev. 1:15). And we understand that it was in the hearing of that voice that John saw Him and became mute before the magnificence.

The mighty voice of our Lord is heard above and beyond the roar of rushing rivers. Yet you and I who love Him have heard that same voice, gentle as a summer breeze, whispering to our weary souls. Oh His voice! He speaks and the sound of His voice is so sweet the birds hush their singing. The melody keeps lingering. So sovereign is His voice that earth trembles, and all therein quake. Yet He deigns to speak sweetly and quietly with me! And when He speaks I see Him! In the hearing comes the seeing!

It has been the prayer of my heart, as these pages were penned, that you too might hear His voice, and in hearing it SEE HIM! May God graciously grant that your faith will strengthen as you hear Him, and your heart discover how to worship when you see Him.

Now we see Him by faith, but soon the glorious day shall dawn when He will appear and we shall see Him as He is. What a moment that will be when for us the Door of Eternity opens and we are called hither to see the great King. Sound and sight will become reality. With batons twirling, and flags unfurling, we shall parade as the innumerable host of those washed

Foreword

white in His precious blood, and all the while the Bands of the Beautiful will play "Amazing Grace". We shall step in unison with faces turned toward Him Who sits high and lifted up, and we shall begin our eternal ovation of praise to Him Who loved us and gave Himself for us; never forgetting for a moment that Wonderful day when we first heard Him speak to us with the voice which is as the sound of many waters.

    Keith E. Knauss

Chapter One

HAPPINESS

"Are you happy?" I could not believe the business man seated across the table had asked such an absurd question. Was he out of his mind? Did he not know we had just moved into new church facilities, boasting a large and luxurious auditorium, with thirty-five new members added the first Sunday, and nearly ten thousand dollars received in the offering! Why I was walking on cloud nine! Yet he had the unmitigated gall to ask if I was happy. Still his question would not go away. It kept probing my mind. Was I really happy?

I sought out the Apostle Paul to confer with him on the matter. I looked him square in the Scripture and asked the same question. "Paul, were you happy?" Did I detect a slight hesitancy? Finally he said, "I have LEARNED in whatsoever state I am, therewith to be content" (Phil. 4:11).

Now Paul, I thought, that is not what I asked you. Don't beat around the bush. I remember what you wrote in Romans chapter seven about feeling wretched. And I have read many times about your perils, stripes, imprisonments and that unceasing Gethsemane of heart. Were you really happy? And would you believe, the closest I ever came to hearing Paul say he was happy was the time he stood before King Agrippa as a prisoner in chains, giving his testimony, and even then he said, "I THINK myself happy" (Acts 26:2).

Let me put the same question to you. Are you happy? Or have you just learned to be content? I asked the lady seated in my study if she was happy. She smiled demurely and replied, "Yes". I would have believed her except for a little tear that welled up in the corner of her eye when she said it.

It is safe to say that very few people know genuine happiness. They may smile and laugh, but it is an exercise in the performing arts. Mark them down as great pretenders Laughter and gaiety are so deceptive, for they easily cover a broken heart or spirit, and bypass signs of discontent and unhappiness.

What is Happiness? Is it an attitude? An emotion? A dream? An illusion? Is it a condition? A result? Can anyone define happiness accurately? It cannot be seen. Science cannot explain it. It cannot be dissected or analyzed. As a matter of fact the Bible seldom uses the word "happy". And the word "happiness" does not occur in our English version at all!

Have you found happiness? Or does this predicament called Life seem one prolonged joke out of which you must get as much amusement as possible while it lasts? Has life become a wearisome, burdensome, cheerless, painful experience, hardly worth the living? Perhaps life seems an enemy of happiness, having become a veritable vale of tears and one long funeral dirge of dead hopes and defeated memories.

When the Bible uses the word "happy" it does so usually in a general sense, such as "Happy is that people whose God is the Lord" (Psalm 144:15). The only thing found in the Old Testament to describe happiness is when a man's quiver is full of children (Psalm 127:5). THEN he is said to be happy! Now that is a happiness most of us cannot afford, nor care to pursue. But I have seen some folks on that basis who must be extremely happy.

While we do not find much happiness in the Bible, we find even less about contentment. For example, only one place in the Bible is the word "contentment" found (I Timothy 6:6). Only a handful of other verses use the word "content". It is therefore obvious that one dare not sit around and wait for happiness or contentment to come. It is something LEARNED! Paul said he had "learned to be content", and that he had been "instructed". Apparently God had given him the lessons several times. In the School of God one of the non-elective courses taught concerns how to be content and happy in this world.

To be happy in the sense Paul speaks of is one of life's greatest victories. Paul got to that place where he MASTERED his circumstances. Though his life was one of constant suffering and trial, he found he could live with his circumstances and experience a peace that passeth all human understanding.

It may be you assume God has been unfair with you. Your prayers and dreams have not known fulfillment. It seems God is liberal with others, while you have a rough road. Perhaps it is because if your path had been smooth you would have depended upon your own surefootedness. If the weather had been mild you would have loitered along the way. But

He sent the storm and you quickened your steps heavenward, and wrapped closer about you the robe of His righteousness.

Be assured that not one thing in this world ever fully satisfies. Any happiness is short lived. Abundance of things does not produce happiness. Only in Him whom we trust is absolute satisfaction, regardless of our situation. He who holds the waters in the hollow of His hand will not allow you to die of thirst. He who owns the cattle on the thousand hills, and all the potatoes therein, will not suffer you to starve.

Early tomorrow morning listen to the joyful singing of the birds, They have had no breakfast, know not where they will lunch at noon, nor have any idea where they will dine in the evening, yet they go on singing. They do not sow, neither do they reap, nor gather in barns, yet your Heavenly Father feedeth them. And are you not more precious to Him than they?

The happiness of the soul is too large a craft to sail up the small stream of this world. Our happiness will run its course on the river of eternity. Happiness is not WHERE you are, or WHAT you have, but WHOSE you are. And we are the children of God! The way we live with that in mind makes one content or miserable with life.

Paul sang while shackled and suffering in a Philippi dungeon. Daniel slept like a baby though faced by a den of lions. The three Hebrew men enjoyed walking and talking with the Son of God amid flames in a fiery furnace. Job lost health, wealth, family, etc., but kept a right spirit. Many a Bible character found himself in situations foreign to happiness, yet in those times drew honey from thistles, and sweetness for the trails, and went on.

Too many find bad in the beautiful, like the spider draws poison from the flowers! But the contented spirit extracts a heavenly nectar from briars and thorns, and discovers the good God had prepared for them there.

We are engaged in constant battle, and it is so intense we have not much time to enjoy any good found in this world. But our time is coming. In the morning joy cometh, and then we shall triumphantly sing and shout and dance about as we enter the joy of the Lord forever. Show vigilance, for the battle is not over. Once again we faced satan this morning, and battled him all the day long; but in our weakness God sent reinforcements, and at sundown we sang victory's song. Yes the sun's coming up in the morning, and every tear will be gone from our eyes. All these griefs will

Happiness

---

give way to glory, and like an eagle we will rise to the skies...released from the cursed cage of this world...FREE AND HAPPY AT LAST!

Chapter Two

WHEN THE JOURNEY IS TOO GREAT

Many who lived in the Chicago area will never forget the blizzard a few years ago when a record snowfall virtually brought the house down. The weight of the snow was so great that over five hundred roofs collapsed; even the roof of a roofing company! Buildings succumbed which appeared built to handle the load.

Today we are witnessing a record breaking of lives. More people are experiencing breakdowns than ever before. Somehow life's journey has gotten too great for them and the inevitable burnout happened, evidenced in physical, mental, or spiritual collapse.

Medical experts inform us that fifty percent of all illness is Emotionally Induced Illness (EII). Incidentally, as far as professional counselors are concerned, there is no such thing as a nervous breakdown. That is the lay term. The problem stems from an overbalance in some area. In fact one of the first things counselors look for is OVERSTRAIN!

That is what Elijah experienced; a collapse from overload. It seems reasonable to assume this when we consider all he went through. Recall in I Kings 18 that he had the emotional trauma of facing the hostile King and delivering God's ultimatum, then becoming a fugitive in hiding for three years; all the while knowing the nation was scouring the country to find and kill him. He came out of hiding to challenge the King, and then alone confronted eight hundred and fifty false prophets of Baal on Mt. Carmel and slew them. It seems he had reached the danger zone. Yet after he prayed and prayed, and the sign of rain appeared, he then ran before the chariot of Ahab all the way to the entrance of Jezreel. That should have done it! He was emotionally, physically, and spiritually exhausted. Perhaps now you can understand the effect that Overstrain, Overwork and Overload had upon Elijah.

As though that were not enough, the phone rang. Surely it was Monday morning. Someone had not agreed with what was said or done

When the Journey is too Great

on Sunday. It was Jezebel on the line, saying, "Preacher, you've had it! You've gone too far! By this time tomorrow your oil will be checked, and your goose cooked. You will be as dead as my prophets you slew. You have just twenty-four hours to get things wrapped up before I do the same to you!"

That was the last straw! It was that extra that collapsed Elijah's roof. The account says, "When he saw that...he went for his life" (I Kings 19:3). When he imagined what she would do to him he broke down. When he got his eyes off God, and on a person and the circumstances, he went for his life. That means he was moving in high gear. All you could see was the Jet Stream! He went the Way of the Wilderness and ruined the work of a lifetime!

You must remember this preacher could run. He had outrun Ahab's horses, and now he runs one hundred fifteen miles to Beersheba. His servant could not keep up, so Elijah left him there and kept on running deeper into the wilderness for another day; and it is hard to run soaking wet for two days in a downpour. Condemn not Elijah, for it is better to run FROM Jezebel than to run AFTER her.

Finally Elijah could run no further and he sat down beneath a juniper tree. It is here many depressed disciples have joined him. He was so down he prayed for God to take his life. Strange he should pray for God to do the dirty work when Jezebel would gladly have done it. Elijah was like so many who are strong on Mt. Carmel, but weak under the Juniper. The overwhelming personal defeat of this stalwart is staggering! He was a man of deep devotion and unquestioning obedience to God, a man of daring faith and true humility. He was built for stress and strain. Nevertheless we see him in spiritual shambles, saying, "It is enough" ("I've had it!").

When we read I Kings 19:4 we are reminded that James said, "Elijah was a man of like passions." He went through what we go through. What produced his depression and defeat may produce ours. He was WORN OUT; having run for three days plus. He was HUNGRY; three days of running with no McDonald stops. He was DISAPPOINTED; nobody had stood with him and he concluded all were against him. He was LONELY; "I only am left." Elijah could hear the countdown of his life and ministry being sounded off. Where had it gotten him?

Is it not wonderful that when Elijah was down God did not yell at him, or kick him? He had something better in store for Elijah. God RESTED him..."He lay and slept." God often lets us sleep awhile when beneath the Juniper. The medical world has discovered the best treatment for collapse is rest. How far behind can they be? They may put a man to sleep for three weeks to bring about recovery. Then God REFRESHED him.."He did eat." God prepared a table for him in the wilderness. He drank of the cruse and ate of the cake (doubtless it was angel food). And God said, "EAT, BECAUSE THE JOURNEY IS TOO GREAT FOR THEE" (I Kings 19:7).

It was as Elijah rested that an angel "touched" him. Oh the tender touches from Heaven. How merciful that God touches our lives in those moments when we feel we are out of it, useless, and nobody caring. That may be your conclusion today. You may be physically, emotionally, and spiritually drained. You may have surpassed your load limit, and to solve the matter you have headed for the obscurity of the wilderness. Even now you find yourself a member of Elijah's Juniper Tree Order. The overload of life has brought collapse of your structure, and you need another touch from God.

God does not condemn you. Instead, when you come to the end of yourself, you find Cake and a Cruse and God Caring for you by touching your life. He cares as much for you as He did for Elijah. In fact you are His constant concern (I Peter 5:7).

In the strength of God's rest and refreshing, Elijah continued on forty more days, or three hundred twenty miles from where he fled from Jezebel. Indeed the journey would have been too great without God's table and touch. Elijah came to Horeb, and a cave where God communed with him in a still small voice. Be assured that no matter how far you journey, God knows your whereabouts and wants, and He never leaves you nor forsakes you. Rest in Him and wait on Him, for He will soon be softly speaking to you. Otherwise the journey is too great.

Chapter Three

THE SOUND OF MANY WATERS

Men little appreciate the beauty that graces their lives through sight. What a blessing it is to see. But have you ever thought of the beauty that is beheld through sound? Double is the blessing when we can see with both eyes and ears.

Many have made the statement that they know a portion of Scripture so well they can walk through it with their eyes closed. That may be true, for even a blind man can tell where he is going when in familiar surroundings. But imagine walking through the familiar portions of God's Word with both ears and eyes giving sight! What one hears can be exquisitely beautiful, for what one hears may unfold a multitude of unforgettable wonders.

A simple sound can produce a myriad of pictures; like the sound of a familiar voice on the phone saying, "It is so good to hear your voice." It is the sound, not the sight, that brings to mind a parade of pleasant memories.

It was so with the apostle John. On Patmos Isle he heard the voice of our Lord and it was like the sound of many waters (Rev. 1:15). It was the perfect concord of divers tones; many waters but one voice. John declared the Lord's voice to be like that of a trumpet, but described it as the melodious merging and mingling of many waters. With the sound came the seeing.

It is true with us. For instance my grandson said, "Grandpa, put this shell to you ear and you can hear the ocean." I did, and sure enough it was so! And in the sound I saw what my eye could not see. I could see the churning of ocean depths, the ceaseless breaking of white capped waves upon rocky shorelines. I could see waves shattering in formless foam on distant reefs; and the surging sea relentlessly driving its forces on. At times the screen of my mind portrayed the thunderous sweeping of waters over mighty Niagara, and that persistent, majestic roaring excluded all other sounds and possessed me. Then it was as though my soul could view the terrible swelling of Jordan as it rolled on to overflow its banks. At

11

times it was as the sound of raging rivers, and then gentle as the falling rain. Again the sound became akin to a whisper, like the tinkle of tiny rivulets cascading in their courses; as soft as the still small voice of God. Yet in the symphony of sounds I saw HIM! And then I understood why it is best that faith cometh by hearing and not by sight, for the soul sees so much more than the eye.

What is the voice of many waters? To John it was the voice of accumulated witness. "God who at sundry times and in divers manners spake in time past unto the fathers by the prophets, hath in these last days spoken unto us by His Son" (Heb. 1:1-2). John could hear the meeting of all the messengers and messages of all time blending and finding fulfillment in Him. Those waters made their way down the hills of long ago in single streams, but all their sources and courses were bent on Him. And in Him they became the heavenly harmony of a million melodies both past and present.

Oh the infinitude of His voice. No man ever spake as He. He speaks and the sound of His voice is so sweet the birds hush their singing; yet it is so sovereign the waves halt their surging.

We may not hear God's voice in the wind as at Pentecost, or in the earthquakes as at Calvary and the Resurrection, or in the fire as at Mount Carmel. Instead we may hear His still small voice while He ministers to us the cruse and cake, as when He communed in the cave with Elijah.

Today men and churches seem sold on sound and size, and too often become discontent with the quiet ways in which God speaks or works, for God may deign to manifest Himself in stillness and smallness. It is beyond argument that often the greatest things make the least noise. The sun draws millions of gallons of water with less noise than some drink a glass of soda through a straw.

Have you ever heard the revolving of the planets, or the falling of the dew? That is how still God may speak. Perhaps we do not hear His voice because our ear is tuned for the wind and not the whisper! Woe unto us if we are so deafened by the whirlwind that we cannot hear the whisper.

Child of God you may be baffled and buffeted but place His precious Word to your heart and hear for yourself the voice which is as the sound of many waters. Like John, you may have to turn to SEE the voice. That voice may come to you in either the power of the Lion or the peacefulness of the Lamb. But however He speaks, it will be in the hearing of His voice that you will SEE HIM! For with the voice will come the vision.

Chapter Four

LONELY ROADS

It is a proven fact! You can take the boy from the country, but you cannot take the country from the boy. Time has removed me from those quiet pastoral places, but this country lad still finds them imbedded deep within his system. I love the lure of country roads. Those lovely scenes, those lonely situations, those lingering silences, still haunt my memory.

Years of walking lonely roads have proven an immeasurable education and preparation, for life has been full of them. Often the road of life has taken sharp turns, made its way through darkened vales, or ascended steep grades, but still it has gone on. Sometimes one can see distant things coming down that road, yet often the unseen and unexpected transpire.

God's people all know lonely roads at times. David could look back over the varied ways his life had taken and say that whether the road took him through green pastures knee deep in grace, by ways of winding waters, or through valleys shrouded in shadows, he feared no evil for his Lord was with him. Despite the problems of the path, he knew he was being led by his Shepherd, and that, regardless of what the way or day brought forth, goodness and mercy were always faithfully and gently prodding him onward and homeward. David discovered the rugged road to also be a pleasant path for God manifested His presence, ministered His annointing oil, and multiplied the bread for his table.

You may be walking an EMMAUS ROAD just now. You walk with head down, for heavy is the heart, and so much is missed that way. Like the two in Luke's Gospel, you walk in despair. Things have not turned out as you thought or hoped. It was so with this couple. The Lord had been crucified and buried and the stone rolled in to seal the tomb. It is now three days later and these discouraged disciples are taking the tiresome trudge from Jerusalem to their home in Emmaus. They are traveling in tears. They should have been singing, instead of sighing. They should have been shouting Hallelujah, instead they are sharing heartache. What should have been their delight has become their despair, for they "had trusted" this "Prophet" to be Messiah. They are living in bitterness instead of blessing. Their faith

Lonely Roads

seemed all in vain.

At least they were willing to talk together about what troubled them. And as they conversed a third Person joined them in their journey. Sweet it is to know Christ walks and talks with the depressed and despairing. And this Comforter of the downcast began at Moses and revealed Himself to them in ALL the Scripture. He "opened the Scripture", "opened their eyes", and "opened their understanding". He disentangled their thinking!

And when they looked back on that wonderful conversation they said, "Did not our hearts burn within us!" It is along the Emmaus Road that He reveals Himself through His Word. And in that journey comes the experience of the burning heart.

Or perhaps today you walk the JERICHO ROAD. All mankind has traveled this road. Along the way sat begging blind Bartimaeus, his hand extended. The nameless man of Luke Ten came "down" this way as he journeyed to Jericho. Like him you have suffered at the cruel hands of others, been left destitute and hurting, bearing undeserved wounds. Like him you may not know there is Another who journeys. He is not going "down". He just journeys, and carries sufficient oil and wine to minister to your needs. He comes to where you lay languishing, and He has compassion on you and concern for you.

Then too, like Paul, you may be traveling a DAMASCUS ROAD. Forces were at work in Paul's life that were driving him in a different direction. He was resisting them; his very breath a response of rebellion. He kicked against God's roads, and the more his heart and conscience were pricked, the more vicious he became. He was like Ghengis Khan, a one-man rampaging army.

Some places along the Damascus Road may stand out forever in your memory, especially that place where you were apprehended of God. It may have been at some quiet bend in the road, or alongside some whispering waterway, or during the heat of a crisis hour, but there He was, and you discovered WHO He is, and confessed Him "Lord".

Our lovely Lord knows all about lonely roads, and about the people who walk them. That is why He knows the way you take, and understands what you are going through. He journeyed the long road from Eternity Past to Bethlehem, and also traveled the lonesome road to Calvary. He knows and understands, and He promises, "I will never leave thee, nor forsake thee". Trust Him, and walk on in faith!

Chapter Five

"OH THAT I WERE AS..."

Sometimes I get the feeling I belong to a bygone era. At least I find myself out of touch and time with this world. It is something like the boy marching in a High School band. He was marching all right, but not in step. Come to find out he had a transistor radio plugged into his ear and was marching to music from elsewhere. I walk out of step with this present world for my heart is harmonizing with music from the homeland, and as I march my mind is lost in the luxury of memories of better days.

Job had a tendency like unto mine. He was able to tolerate his situation a little by reverting to memory, and thus a prayerful sigh escaped his lips, "Oh that I were as in months past, as in days WHEN..." (Job 29:2). Walking down memory's lane he recalled the days when God kept him, communed with him, was the light of his life, gave him the energy and zeal of youth, and life seemed rich and the sailing always smooth... "I washed my steps with butter"! Then he placed the crown of life on it all by adding, "When my children were about me".

Those were wonderful days! We thought they would never end. Mother always said the best time of life was when the children were about her. We have come to understand what she meant. What joy it was to watch those precious personalities sitting about the table, hear their lilting laughter throughout the house, and watch their constant development. Those were the days for it seemed God spread the canopy of contentment over us, that He was everywhere evident. Now the ghost of Christian Past laughs at us from a distance.

This heart feels like Jeremiah's at times, and longs for a return to the old paths and old ways. When we look at the status quo in our churches today we also sigh the supplication for days WHEN. It is not the problem of the world that bothers us, but the plight of the churches. The wood is set in order, but there is no fire. We have come to the place where folks mistake Rigor Mortis for dignity! In many churches one sits through a frenzy of evangelistic epilepsy, and comes away feeling like they had been to a carnival instead of a church. We depart wondering what

"Oh That I Were As..."

happened to the good old days, and praying as Isaiah did, "Oh that thou wouldest rend the heavens...and come down...as WHEN" (Isa.64:1-2).

Oh for the days of WHEN. Days when God seemed to walk among us and touch us. Days when folks prayed on their knees. Days when you did not have to explain what a Revival was. The memories of some special days caress my thoughts with pleasantness, and I long to see them repeated. Like the days when preaching in little country churches in the Missouri foothills, where people crowded into the buildings and latecomers would stand outside and listen through open windows. I recall one meeting where a giant of a man, who would not have been caught dead inside a church, stood outside and heard the truth. The Sword of the Lord smote him hip and thigh, soul and spirit, from outset to outcome, until he fell on his face before God begging for mercy. And God not only saved him but called him to preach.

Those were the days when the amazing "Amen Corner" was alive and active. And sometimes shrapnel got to flying shot-gun style in every direction, and satan and his cohorts would flee for refuge. And if more support was needed the double barreled big guns were rolled out, the powder lit, and a heavy barrage of Hallelujah and Praise the Lord volleyed forth to fill the air and set the service on fire. The Shekinah Glory settled in and what a meeting was had! The mourner's bench would fill, and there was heard the singing and shouting of Victory. Nowadays folks come to the altar, but they are not "mourners".

Asaph experienced feelings akin to ours. His life seemed to veer from the day of blessing to the day of bitterness. He sought the Lord long into the night, but no comfort came. He complained to God, his spirit overwhelmed. He thought back on the good old days WHEN he had a song in the night; but now there was no song to sing. He compared the present to the past and concluded God had forgotten and forsaken him, or was angry with him.

Then Asaph came to his spiritual senses, and said, "THIS IS MY INFIRMITY" (Psa. 77:10). He realized that life never stays the same, only God. He changeth not. It was then Asaph said, "I will remember the years of the right hand of the Most High...I will remember the works of the Lord...I will remember the wonders of old...I will meditate on thy work...and talk of thy doings". He determined to forget the "days of old" and dwell on the "years" (or eternity) of the Most High. He would get his mind off himself, and onto God. He would no longer think of WHEN, but of THEN...the unchanging eternity!

You can appreciate Asaph if you have ever spent time in the Dumps, or had spells of the Blues. Most of our down moments result from a complaining spirit. It was true of Asaph. In the first half of his Psalm he thought only of himself. In the second half he thought only of God. He realized God was not to blame for his attitude. He understood that dwelling on the past can become an INFIRMITY! So he set his mind on things above.

That is how Job overcame. He discovered the WHEN was an infirmity, and the THEN was an incentive. Job had been reduced to the point of being a stranger to his wife. Little children mercilessly mocked him at his manifest misery. Closest friends abhorred him, and loved ones turned against him. His bones clave to his skin, and he knew he was holding onto life only by the skin of his teeth. He looked at the clay potsherd in his hand, then at the skin hanging down from his bones, and the witness of faith assured him the best was yet to come.

The confession of Job at that moment came from a man who was looking past THEN to WHEN. Though appearing as the off-scouring of humanity, Job sat on that dunghill like a despot on his throne. He rose a ruler of the ruins to triumphantly declare, "I know that my Redeemer liveth, and that He shall stand at the latter day upon the earth; and though after my skin worms destroy this body" (and here I think Job broke forth with the laughter of faith) "YET IN MY FLESH SHALL I SEE GOD" (Job 19:25-26). When by faith Job saw himself redeemed before God, the grievous immediate was swallowed up in the glorious inevitable, and he saw nothing but the THEN.

Now that blessed hope places us with Paul in a strait betwixt two (Phil. 1:23).While in many ways we wish we were as in the days of WHEN, we also wish we were as in the days of THEN! Our Lord is coming at any moment to catch His bride away. THEN the trumpet will sound, THEN we which are alive and remain shall be caught up together with them to meet the Lord in the air...THEN this mortal shall put on immortality...THEN this corruptible shall put on incorruption...THEN shall be brought to pass the saying that is written, "Death is swallowed up in victory"...THEN shall I wake in His likeness...THEN shall I see Him as He is...THEN shall I know as I am known!

Oh that I were as...THEN!

Chapter Six

BEYOND THE VISIBLE

The secret of emancipation is in seeing the unseen. The slave is he who never looks past his fetters. The truly free man, whatever his state in this world, is the one who endures because he beholds that which is beyond the visible.

Man cannot see much with his eyes, not because they are bad, but because they are not built to behold the invisible and the infinite. With his eyes he can only touch the surface, and shadow, the temporary, the changing, the things which do appear. If he is to rise in companionship with God he must seek the permanent, the abiding, the everlasting, the invisible. He must look not with his eyes but with his soul.

It is not fanciful imagination that seeing and enduring are twined together inseparably. There is a great cloud of witnesses that share this testimonial of faith. True faith lifts its eyes unto the hills, views the horizon, and sees God in and behind all. How shameful the indictment written against Israel, "They turned back...and limited the Holy One" (Psalm 78:41). They placed limits on the limitless God! The word "limited" is better translated "horizoned". In other words, Israel trusted God only so far as they could humanly see. They lived with faith out of focus, and so in unbelief retreated before the foe and became slaves to a situation.

The Earthbound behold a horizon just twenty six miles away! Imagine God, whom the heavens cannot contain, being held to such fleshly confines of sight. On the other hand the Seafaring find the oceanic horizon a mere nine and a half miles away! Thus when in deep waters the unbelieving find themselves in danger of reducing the Almighty to a nautical nothing. However, the Heavenbound press onward, and in so doing find the horizon limitless and God becoming greater and greater.

If a man of God would accomplish the impossible he must of necessity see the invisible. Like Moses who looked with his soul and endured by seeing Him who is invisible (Heb. 11:27). As he gazed enrapt

Beyond the Visible

upon the unseen his heart beat faster, and because he saw the invisible he rejected the immediate to gain the imperishable. By faith he turned his back on the pomp and power and plenty of the palace and set his face like a flint toward the distant horizon. He had taken the look that lasts, and that look made the difference.

The man of God is under divine complusion to press on, and as he proceeds in the walk of faith the horizon keeps retreating and expanding. Such men see in those horizons what others cannot. Moses held such a vision, and it made him the maker of an age, the creator of a civilization, the leader of a nation, the shepherd of a people. He looked beyond the brickkilns, beyond the bondage, beyond the oppression, beyond the impossible, beyond the invisible, and saw emancipation. He saw the light of Canaan in the far horizon and it made him a free man. He broke through conventionalism, threw down worldly ambition, defied Egypt, and began walking out of the Midian Wilderness to climb mountains, and stride through seas, all the while beset by the baffling onslaughts of the enemy of faith.

Elisha was such a man. He looked beyond material barriers and caught the vision of the unseen. He saw readied armies and flaming chariots. Such men discover, not that which is, but that which can be and is to be. Their souls are aglow with the ecstasy of a sight no mortal eye has ever seen. It is not what one sees in a picture that makes it great; it is what they do not see. The rapturous quality of a song is not what one hears, it is what is not heard. The divine realm is ever beyond the reach of the sense. Only he can invade it who has a soul that sees.

Abraham was spiritually far-sighted and pioneered the pathway of faith. In his heart was cradled the vision that prompted him to forsake kindred and country and press on in a pilgrimage to seek the City Celestial, whose builder and architect was God. He viewed many earthly horizons along that pilgrim way but kept journeying on. Such men are not satisfied until they reach the heavenly horizon, where the sun neither rises nor sets and the day is eternally fragrant and fadeless.

In the life of faith you will walk through sunshine and shadow, share your lot of tears and triumphs, experience untold heartache and happiness, but you will learn to walk always with an eye to the horizon; the horizon of the coming day. In that day the invisible will give way to the visible., the shadow will give way to substance, and we shall behold and hold Him as He is. May the shadows quickly flee away.

Chapter Seven

"HE RESTORETH MY SOUL"

How wonderful to know that the God who Redeems is also the God who Restores. He is the God of the second opportunity, and the third, and the seventy times seven. Frail and failing man can always begin afresh with the God of all grace.

Too often we make our stumbling, sinful way down into Egypt, and God always waits for us to return. He allows the difficulties that occur in Egypt to make us long for the bread of His table and the blessings of His communion. Far country swine husks are but the hors d'oeuvres before the fatted calf and the full course of restoration.

In Abraham we are provided the story of a man who possessed riches and grew to despise them. He came to rely wholly on the Restorer of his soul. God's dealings with Abraham are a pattern of what we may expect from our Heavenly Father. Like Abraham many remain out of God's will for lengthy periods of time. That is why God has given us such minute details of the process of his restoration. Even Abraham, father of the faithful, sinned to his own hurt and the harm of others. But always the God of all grace was ever ready to restore him.

No painter of any period of time could have drawn such a portrait as has the inspired penman of the man called David. No other life in all history has been portrayed in almost every conceivable predicament. What a priceless legacy left us in the gallery of Scripture. Every child of God should be thankful for the unvarnished record of David's life. There are none who can discount his greatness. Yet, like ourselves, David occasionally went astray only to be brought back by the firm but gracious hand of the Great Shepherd of the sheep.

It would seem God wanted to show His people, through the example of David, that the loftiest sainthood does not save from temptation, nor free from the laws of retribution. David could be so rich in spiritual life one moment, and so reckless in sin the next. Yet only those who have worshipped with his fervor, praised with his ecstasy, sinned with his

"He Restoreth My Soul"

abandon, and repented with his contrition, can see through the lattice of his checkered career the merciful dealings of God in restoring him. David reveals to us the heights to which a sinner may be raised and depths to which a saint may sink.

It is to David that we owe the comforting words, "He restoreth my soul" (Psalm 23:3). The old Saxton translation renders it, "He keeps bringing back my soul." Amen and Amen! This old nature we live with is so bent to sinning, so prone to straying, so easily pinned to the canvas with depression, that if God did not lift us up and restore us to life and fellowship we would lay right where we fell.

No wonder God likened us to sheep. It is common for sheep to roll over on their back and lay there until they die, for a sheep cannot get back on its feet without help. A sheep needs continual shepherding. And we need continual shepherding for we keep going astray. It may be by chastening or comforting, but God blends correction with tenderness and keeps giving our life back to us.

"He restoreth my soul"! David meant that the Lord keeps him going. Have you ever been downcast and needed help? The term "cast" comes from animal husbandry. A cast sheep is one that may have eaten his fill of the green pastures and then rested next to a hollow in the ground into which he rolled onto his back. Downcast is being in a condition in which you cannot roll back onto your feet. David said his SOUL was downcast! He remembered all the times in his life when he had been spiritually on his back, his life and soul paralyzed, and each time the Lord restored him and got him going again.

"He restoreth my soul"! The hand which rescued us from ruin, now reclaims us in restoration. He restores our soul to its original purity. What good is it to have green pastures and a black soul! When the soul is sorrowful He comforts it; when it is defiled He cleanses it; when it is wrong He corrects it. HE does it! We can not do it. He who turns the ebb into a flood, will restore the dried and barren life and refill it to overflowing.

Chapter Eight

MINISTERING

Surely there is no greater joy experienced by the servant of God than preaching to those who listen with face aglow as though they were reveling in a great discovery, or rolling a choice morsel around their tongue while savoring every goodness of that delicacy.

Such a person has come often to graciously say, "Pastor, you just minister to me". The expression "minister", like a seed in the soil of meditation, brought forth the realization that is precisely the way it ought to be. God has indeed given us such a ministry. Paul verified it, saying, "We have this ministry" (II Cor. 4:1). It is a ministry like unto our Lord's.

Our lovely Lord came not to be ministered unto, but to minister (Mark 10:45), and we as His undershepherds must understand our calling is a life-long servantship to others. Like our Lord who, when He blessed and broke the little loaves, gave to the disciples and they in turn ministered to the multitude and the hungry were fed and filled. We are not only Seed-Sowers, and Light-Bearers, but Bread-Passers.

The hurting of heart are hungry, and the sinners of Sychar are thirsting, and they have need to be ministered unto. That may necessitate going out of our way to touch their lives at the very wells from which they draw. It may mean the throwing out of the life line to those adrift on wind-swept waters. It may mean, like Paul, becoming all things to all men that, by all means, we might save some. Oh to be like Him Who is able to minister to every need of failing man.

That wonderful One Who ministers to men is the Sovereign Succorer, the ministering Melchizedek, Who bringeth forth bread and wine to refresh the Abrahams battling the forces of this world amid the slime pits in the vale of Siddim. On that dark background the Sovereign from Salem, in anticipation of the death of Christ, ministered bread and wine to the war weary Abraham and blessed him; and in the strength of that ministration the pilgrim of faith plodded on in his journey through Immanuel's land to find the beautiful City of God.

That wonderful One is also the Shepherd of the Sheep, Who ministers by preparing a table in the wilderness, and in so doing supports His flock as they walk through darksome valleys and experience dangerous encounters with the enemies lurking round about. And upon His merciful ministration the eye of faith lifts and looks beyond the inexplainable to view the eternal, and the Father's House.

That wonderful One is the Servant of the Sanctuary, Who takes basin and towel in hand, and, as the Living Laver, ministers cleansing to His defiled disciples.

That wonderful One is the Sweet Saviour of Sinners, Who ministers restoration and recovery to penitent prodigals and so mingles the human into the divine.

Always it seems we have believed the prodigal son made his wandering way back home alone. No, the father went after him! The father was waiting and watching, and at the very moment the sinning son breathed the blest words, "I will arise and go to my father", that is when the quantum leap was made and the chasm spanned between the two. Then it says, "when he was YET a great way off", or when he was yet the same distance away as he had gone into the far country, that is when the father met him. At the very instant repentance was found in the heart and mind of the sinful son, the father ran to meet and embrace him. Would you believe, this is the only time in Scripture where God is seen in a hurry! How quick He is to minister.

The Prodigal was driven to repentance by hunger! In his great gnawing need he remembered the father's house had "bread enough and to spare". Oh the need of bread, or of JESUS, that drives men home to God.

And how abundantly was the Prodigal ministered unto when that break in his insanity came and he repented. No sooner had he breathed his desire but the father was immediately there to throw about him the arms of compassion, and to render the royal kiss of reconciliation. Then was freely ministered the Robe, the Ring, the Shoes, and the Feast. There was bestowed upon the prodigal a new sense of his Standing, his Sonship, his Service, and the Satisfaction which only our loving God can minister. Then began the ministry of music! And such "an entrance shall be ministered unto you" (II Peter 1:11).

Chapter Nine

COMING HOME

Old fashioned homecomings have become a thing of the past. Family reunions used to be the gala event of summer. Folks showed up who had not been back home in years. Women hugged each other and cried. Men clasped hands, slapped each other on the shoulder and said, "It is good to be home." Children stared at each other, then ran off to play. Tables were laden with bounty befitting a king and his court. To this boy the chicken legs looked big as a man's fist, huge biscuits were busting out over the rims of the tins, and five-layered cakes made the eyes large with longing. We ate and laughed and loved and knew the thrill of being family and being home.

In thinking over material blessings we would have to list Home at the top. Like the hymn writer phrased it, "Thanks for home and thanks for fireside..." There was always that special feeling when I could say to my children, or hear them say, "Let's go home." Home is the place where you can hang both your head and your hat, and still be accepted. Home is the place of security, contentment, refreshment, and freedom. Our youngest daughter never wanted to stay overnight anywhere as a child. When asked why, she said, "Because you can't go to the refrigerator before you go to bed." It is true, be it ever so humble there is no place like home.

Home has entwined itself about our hearts and minds. Ever since Adam was driven from Eden, man has dreamed of home and longed to go back. Jacob lived a life far from commendable. He swindled his brother out of the family inheritance; cheated his father-in-law of most of his assets, but he never forgot his beginnings. Finally he gathered his family about him and said, "I'm tired of living this way, we are going home." And back to Bethel they went. Back home to where God was. Back home where happiness had its address.

David, when graced with years, looked back over his life and remembered the shady green pastures, the winding paths, the still waters, the dark valleys, God's anointing and provision, the daily guardianship of Goodness and Mercy, and saw beyond his today to God's tomorrow, and home...the home he would never leave again...the Home of Forever.

Jerry MacCauley was drunk and staggering toward a bridge in New York City with suicide on his mind, when through the cacophonous sounds of the city came singing from a nearby mission, "Come ye sinners lost and hopeless, Jesus' blood can make you free. For He saved the worst among you, when He saved a wretch like me." MacCauley turned about and said, "I'm going home!"

The Prodigal Son made his wandering way to the Far Country, wasting both life and substance, but the thought of home was ever present with him. It was the remembrance of the blessings of home that made him turn around. When he thought of the smell and taste and plentitude of the bread in the Father's House he turned his back on the Hog Lot and said, "I'm going home." Home is where music is heard, love is known, and blessing is experienced.

It is to Luke we are indebted for portraying The God Of The Outstretched Arms. God is seen as always receiving sinners. Luke provides such unforgettable accounts as the Samaritan helping the unloved man on Jericho's Road, the repentant Publican standing afar off, the blind beggar crying out for mercy, the grieving widow beside the bier, the dying thief, Zacchaeus, etc.. This truth seems to reach its zenith in chapter fifteen where the Pearl of Parables sets forth the joy over lost sinners coming home. Here the story of the Prodigal Son comes into focus.

The Prodigal Son wanted freedom from the Father. To do as he pleased he left home. You know the rest of the story. He started out in his best togs, went to the dogs, wound up with the hogs, and finally homeward jogs. It is that coming home which provides the highlight. What love and restoration is found. What joy and grace he experienced. What sumptuous feasting was prepared. There is nothing like coming home.

Perhaps you are like the prodigal, far from home. You have been hiding in the hog lot of the far country, wondering if you dare come home; wondering if God would forgive you, receive and restore you. Oh, He will! He is looking your way even now, waiting for you to make that first move homeward.

Take a moment to read the personal story of a prodigal daughter. A young woman fled from home fearing parents would discover her wrong doing. In God's good grace she journeyed westward, and by chance knocked at our parsonage door. Upon learning she was with child, without room or money, my wife welcomed her with an embrace. She was a stranger and we took her in.

Days moved into weeks and finally the weight of guilt became more than she could bear. We heard the outpouring of an anguished soul as she began to freely talk of what was bothering her. Imaginations besieged her mind as to what her folks would think or do, should they know of her sin. We urged her to write or phone them. She steadfastly refused, insisting they could not love her after what she had dome, that they would hate her, disown her, write her off forever.

Finally my wife suggested writing home but not telling her parents where she was, just letting them know she was alive and well; for they deserved to know that. At last the barriers broke down, and the tear stained letter was written. But the penitent prodigal went beyond what was suggested and penned the whole story. She told them she knew they could not possibly love her after what she had done, BUT if they still did love her, and could forgive her, to be at the Burlington Station in Ottumwa, Iowa, on such a day and at a certain time. She sent the letter convinced they would not care enough to come.

On the designated day we arrived at the station one half hour early, and parked our car. Would you believe her folks, having driven from another state, were already there and waiting. She could see them parked five car lengths away. The young lady was trembling so much she could hardly work the door handle. Would you believe when she got out of the car the whole family was already running towards her. Mom was racing like a march wind, tears rolling unchecked down her face, and with both arms wide open. She outsped them all to reach the daughter first, and the prodigal child fell into those arms. Little sister got there next and reached in to clinch both arms about the waist. Dad gathered them all into his huge arms and they stood there and swayed back and forth, and cried and kissed, cried and kissed. Oh the kissing! My wife and I, watching it all from our car, sat there and bawled like babies. We were seeing a prodigal come home and be restored. Luke Fifteen had come alive.

Oh how God loves us. That is how He loves you. He will run to meet you if you will but start homeward. I can verify this truth; I know there is nothing like coming home! Many of us have made our way back to God with these words being wrung from our hearts, "Lord, I'm coming home!"

Chapter Ten

GOD'S FINEST HOUR!

It is said when England was rocking and reeling beneath the devastating blows of German bombing, and a full invasion appeared imminent, that Prime Minister Winston Churchill delivered England's Gettysburg Address. He spoke by radio to the battered nation and said, "We shall fight them in the air and on the sea, we shall fight them in the fields and in the streets, we shall fight them with sticks and stones, we shall fight them as long as we have breath left in our bodies." And then amid tears and trembling, and with deep emotion, he cried, "We shall never surrender, and it will be said that this was England's finest hour!" And so it was!

What was God's finest hour? When was God at His best? What was God's greatest work? The Psalmist said that God's works are wonderful, and beyond numbering (Psalm 40:5). Is it possible then that one of God's works is more wonderful than another, more wonderful than all?

Immediately someone declares Creation to be God's greatest work. And it would be difficult to argue the point when we consider the heavens and the earth. Why the handiwork of God is absolutely awesome. He spoke and innumerable stars graced the spaces. He just said the word and dry land appeared. Oh the wonders our God hath wrought.

Earth alone holds one spellbound with grandeur. To see the endless jagged snow capped Alps, or to stand in the quiet loneliness of a vast desert, or to view the complete circle of the horizon from the midst of an ocean, or to travel through the rolling prairielands where the Blue and Grama grass tickle the underside of a horse, or to smell the fragrance of the fruited plains, or to listen to the whispering of the forested pines, makes all that is within you break forth into singing, "My God how great thou art!"

Heaven is unimaginable with the glory of God. To consider the heavens makes one wonder how Abraham kept from staggering at the promise of God. How vast it is. It must go on forever! In 1975 the United

God's Finest Hour!

States put Voyager II into space and fourteen years and four and a half million miles later it sailed past distant Neptune! Scientists said it would then leave our solar system and sail on into inter-space, with enough atomic power left to travel on for forty years! After that they said we would have to go by faith! The heavens are endless in immensity!

Neptune's moon, Triton, travels on a course that is the reverse of every known moon in the solar system. Could it be that God made it that way as though to say to proud man, "Now figure that one out, if you can!"

If ingenious man found it possible to hollow out the sun, they could place our earth and moon in it and there would still be enough room so the two would remain the same revolving distance apart as they are now. And the sun is one of the smallest balls of fire in the universe!

Who can list, in order of their greatness, the wonderful works of God? True, His work of Creation was one of the greatest. But the work of Redemption was surely greater. And in what class of Greatness would be placed the Incarnation, the Resurrection, the building of His Church, etc.?

Let all guesswork cease, for the greatest work of God happened but a few years ago. As the crow flies and the wheel turns, it took place about five miles northeast of Belvidere, Illinois, down along the bottomlands of the Piscasaw river country. There the Saviour of sinners came walking with omnipotent stride through the cornfields toward an old farm, and stopped down at the hog lot.

It was there the all-righteous God humbled Himself and reached down with tender hands into the muck and mire and pulled this pathetic prodigal from the pit. He put His strong and loving arms around me, washed my heart and mind and mouth and made me clean. A miracle of grace occurred when He took up residence in this vile body and placed a song in this songless life. He gave me His very nature, promised to come back for me and take me to the Father's house, and to make me like Himself!

Oh the grace God revealed when He saved me. What a day! Oh happy day! It made mother cry and angels rejoice! On that day this cursed man became a child of the Everlasting Father. This sinner was Justified, Sanctified, Glorified! This offscouring of all things was made holy! This alien from lower space was granted full citizenship in heaven. This destitute man became an heir of God, and a joint heir with Christ, and his inheritance was reserved in the Bank of Heaven where it fades not away and draws the highest interest.

The rags of ruin were removed and I was clothed in the righteousness of Christ. Then the merciful God lifted me up and seated me in Christ Jesus at His own right hand. That day I became a crown jewel of the King of Kings! And then in wondrous marvelous grace God said to this worthless piece of clay, "Go preach!" Can you believe it!

Someone may accuse God of having been hard put to save the likes of Keith Knauss, and then to call him to preach. That may be, but I can tell you that the day God saved this chief of the chiefs of sinners, it took a miracle of love and grace! And as far as I am concerned it was God's greatest work! It was when God was at His very best! It was God's finest hour!

Chapter Eleven

THE DEPTHS OF HIS LOVE

A little four year old girl standing on the edge of the Grand Canyon, said to her grandfather as they looked down into the mile-deep abyss, "Grandpa, what happened? It is so deep!"

Likewise we stand on the edge of the divine deep, along the shoreline of the ocean of God's love and grace and riches, and utter the same exclamation, "What happened? It is so deep!" Paul's awed response is, "They are past finding out!" That means those depths are immeasurable, undefinable.

It is said that when Nanson was at the North Pole he tried to sound the ocean depths. Each day he would put anchors on long ropes and lower them for thousands of feet. Each night his men would reel in the ropes to judge the measurement. At the end of each day Nanson would write in his log book, "DEEPER THAN THAT!" The next day he would repeat the process of depth preception and write his conclusion, "DEEPER THAN THAT". Finally, frustrated over never being able to ascertain the depths, he made a final entry, "DEEPER THAN THAT!" When all his abilities and resources had been exhausted, he concluded that the ocean depths of the North Pole were beyond knowing.

The love of God for sinners is also beyond human comprehension. We can only stand amazed on the edge of the fathomless deep that stretches from everlasting to everlasting. The wisdom and ways of God are unsearchable. His love and grace are unmeasurable.

We travel to Bethlehem and the stable to witness the miracle of the ages, the INCARNATION! God is housed in flesh! One is born Who is as old as His Father, and ages older than His mother! David's Lord has become David's Son! How deep is such love that causes God to give His only Begotten Son? How deep is God's love that encompasses a world and makes Him offer Himself so that none should ever perish? We employ every known means of measurement to estimate the degree of the depth of that love, and when every system of measurement at our disposal is exhausted, we cry, "IT IS DEEPER THAN THAT!"

We follow the multitude up to Golgotha's rugged crown and view the CRUCIFIXION. There God personifies and displays the Mercy Seat. There the accumulated sins of man, past present and future, are laid upon that Holy Sacrifice. There God gives His only Son to die for the sins of the world. How deep is that love? Again we put to work every system of linear measurement in an attempt to learn the depths of that love. Every means fails, and we can only log our amazed, "IT IS DEEPER THAN THAT!"

We move on to the Garden and bow in wonderment over His death and burial. God died for us! Thoughtless men believed the Light of the World had been extinguished forever! But on that third day, just like the Scripture had foretold, He rose triumphant from the dead, and our hearts were held spellbound at the RESURRECTION! He who had become silent as a sheep before His shearers has conquered sin, and death, and hell! How deep is love that would cause the Altogether Lovely One to give Himself for me, and rise from death for my JUSTIFICATION? Once more we employ caliphers and calculus to determine the depths of that love. And when every means of measurement known to man has failed we conclude we have been wading in the shallows of those waters, and we record our findings with the words, "IT IS DEEPER THAN THAT!"

Then on that rapturous day, when beyond the tides of time I am ushered into the presence of Him Who is the Heretofore, the Herewith, and the Henceforth, and stand before the Throne of the God of Forever, which the emerald rainbow encircles, I shall then behold the blessed Lamb of God in GLORIFICATION. Then I shall realize in reality that all His glory is also all mine, for I shall be standing before Him in His likeness! Then I shall fall prostrate before Him as did John the Seer of Patmos, and I shall cry, HOW DEEP IS LOVE LIKE THIS?

It may be that all the redeemed may forever try to measure that love, and in our futile efforts to determine its depths, may travel to the far side of eternity. And after ten thousands of years have rolled by, and we have experienced the unimaginable lavishness of love, all the while being immortal and incorruptible like He is, we will still not have been able to judge the depths of His great love. And though we took the sands of the sea, and adding them up, multiplied them by the number of the stars in the heavens, we would yet come miserably short of determining the depth and glory of God's love. And should all the blood-washed of all time put their findings together, their conclusive cry would be, "God's love is DEEPER THAN THAT!" For His love passeth knowledge!

Chapter Twelve

THE MYSTERY OF GODLINESS

The Crib, like the Cross, has always been a stumbling block to unbelief. To the attentive reader of the gospel records, He who was born in a manger remains a paradox; for Christ, while absolute God, is truly man. In the prologue of John's Gospel, he sums up all the glory of Eternity and the Nativity by saying, "In the beginning was the Word, and the Word was God...and the Word was made flesh and dwelt among us..." Boiled down, it simply means that the eternal God became man!

Unregenerate minds, however, stumble over this thrilling truth of Incarnation. They cannot discern how God could come into this world by way of a virgin, and so clothe Himself with humanness. Yet the prophets of old foretold that this Messiah of the manger would indeed be none other than the Almighty God, the Everlasting Father, the Ancient of Days! He was not a creation! He was not "a god!" He was and is the Almighty God come in flesh! And John later adds that if any preach or believe otherwise they are deceivers and Antichrist (II John 7).

Men look at the Cross and stumble over the truth that God HIMSELF died for man's sin (though God personally told Abraham it would thus be!) In like manner, men look at the Crib and stumble over the truth that God HIMSELF became incarnate, became virgin-born, and became clothed in flesh. "Without controversy, great is the mystery of godliness, God was manifest in the flesh." (I Tim. 3:16).

Do you stumble over that? Do you believe that in that incomparable infant of Bethlehem lay housed all the attributes of the Godhead? Paul assured us of that when God moved him to write, "In Him dwelleth ALL THE FULLNESS of the godhead bodily." (Col. 2:9).

Place the seed of an Empire apple in your hand. Would you believe within that tiny seed are held all the necessary attributes of an apple tree? It not only holds within itself another Empire apple tree, but the size, shape, color, taste and perpetuation of that tree.

Now place in your other hand the egg of a Rhode Island Red chicken.

Would you believe that within that fragile shell are hoarded all the qualities and characteristics of its species? It contains the habits, the plumage, the structure, the color, the cackle, and the continuation of its kind.

Now look into the manger of Bethlehem. See that lovely Babe there. Believe it or not, but hidden within that frail frame are all the attributes of God! In that body dwells all the fullness of God, for He is God! Housed in Him is the fullness of Omnipotence, Omniscience, Wisdom, Righteousness, Grace, Love, etc., etc. What mystery that God should choose to manifest Himself in the likeness of man! Selah (think of that)!

Unless Jesus Christ be virgin born, all other things are naught. Forget Calvary, ignore the Tomb, write off the Resurrection, for everything is void and valueless unless the incarnation be as the inerrant Scriptures so declare. Might as well put a halt to the preaching of the gospel that Christ DIED, and was BURIED, and ROSE again the third day according to the Scriptures, if Christ be not very God in flesh!

Of the twelve mysteries presented in the Word of God, the mystery of God manifest in the flesh is declared to be the GREAT one! The Virgin Birth is the Monarch of Miracles, the Sovereign of Signs, The Diadem of Doctrines, the Gem of all Graces. It is the foundation stone of Christianity. The weight of Redemption rests squarely upon the blessed bedrock.

Stand forth on the front porch of Scripture and hear the Virgin Birth foretold (Gen. 3:15). Stroll through the ivoried hallways of Scripture and behold the promise form into fulfillment. Stand again at the back door of Scripture and discover that the One who was the WORD before time began, and who was the WORD became flesh during time, is at the close of time, the Coming Conqueror astride a white horse and still called "THE WORD OF GOD" (Rev. 19:13).

Thus, on that Christmas morning in Bethlehem town there commenced the greatest drama of the ages. It was the conclusion of a predetermined plan, made by the Godhead before the foundation of the world. It was the culmination of centuries of loving overtures on the part of God. Oh the mystery of godliness, God was manifest in the flesh!

Chapter Thirteen

ALTOGETHER LOVELY

It has been said that the major sin of man is exaggeration. That may be true, but go ahead and heap praise upon praise to Jesus Christ and you will never be charged guilty of exaggeration. Lay your tongue to every adjective, adverb, prase, paragraph, and superlative in every language known to man, and if you can lay hold on the tongues of angels speak in them too, and you will have only begun to reach out to touch the hem of His loveliness.

Jesus Christ is the only person of whom, without gross flattery, it can be said, "He is altogether lovely". All other greatness has been marred, all other wisdom has been flawed, all other goodness has been stained by imperfection. He alone is worthy of praise.

No mind in any race or realm possesses the capacity to describe, or the capability to declare the multi-glories of the Son of God. His might and majesty are inconceivable. Solomon said, "The heaven and heaven of heavens cannot contain thee" (I Kings 8:27). If the heavens cannot contain Him, how think ye the mind of mortal man can do so? We may search literature and lexicons, histories and homilies, dictionaries and declarations, encyclicals and encyclopedias, only to discover that "no mortal can with Him compare!"

Saints of the ages have gathered the precious pollen of Christ from many plants and places, and drank of the sweet nectar of this Rose of Sharon and Lily of the Valleys until their soul seemed unable to hold more. We all may drink unashamed of this Fountain. It is your right as joint-heir of all He is and has. Drink and you will find yourself full to overflowing, and still thirsting for more and more of Him.

Solomon in all his searching spoke the heart of God's people when he said, "I find no spot in thee." And Pilate spoke for the world when he confessed, "I find no fault in Him." When the Shulamite of Solomon's Song was asked to tell why she thought her beloved was more than any other she delivered a ten-fold discourse describing in detail his beauties from head to foot, and then stopped, as though realizing she could go on forever, and summed it all up in five words, "YEA, HE IS ALTOGETHER LOVELY" (Song of Solomon 5:16).

To attempt to delve into the depths of His loveliness is only to discover the shortness of our plumb line. His loveliness is an ocean so exceedingly broad that our small boats seem driven far out of sight of land, and our spirits tremble to spread the sails any fuller. But rejoice in that if we cannot attain the ocean, we can bathe along the shoreline. If we cannot describe Him, we can at least gaze upon him. We may not be able to gain the bounty of His beauty, but we can gather the tidbits that fall from His table. Hungry men are glad for crumbs, and crumbs from such a feast are better than the loaves of this world. Far better to have a glimpse of Jesus than to see all the glories of earth and miss it.

"He is altogether lovely!" Make each letter of those words with sparkling gems. Use a sapphire, and ruby, a diamond, a pearl. No, for they are perishables! Spirit of God take the fleshly tablets of our minds and hearts and engrave on them the letters of those words. Burn them into our hearts with a live coal from off the altar of heaven. Cleanse our eyes until they become as dove's eyes by the rivers of waters, that we may see nothing but our Lord and His loveliness. May we be so absorbed with Him that we pass into a state of rapture, our hearts burning within, making us mount up with wings as eagles, our souls becoming like the chariots of Amminidab, until like Paul, we experience what we cannot express, finding Him absolutely UNSPEAKABLE!

Oh frail man, bow low before Him in worship. So majestic and lovely is He that even the seraphim cover their faces. Their perpetual anthem being, "HOLY, HOLY, HOLY IS THE LORD OF HOSTS." When Ezekiel and John, the Seers of the Testaments, beheld Him, they fell as paralyzed on their faces. When Jacob met Him at river Jabbok he cried out in both anguish and adoration, "How dreadful is this place! It is the Gate of Heaven" (Gen. 28:17)! When Isaiah saw Him high and lifted up he became undone. He went to pieces! But what he saw changed him forever! The downcast pair walked the Emmaus Road and knew not the One who traveled with them was their lovely Lord, yet their hearts were SET ON FIRE just to see Him in the Scriptures; and you and I can identify with that.

Would you believe that John provided us the only description of our

Lord found in the Bible. It is the picture as He is seen today! John had known Jesus all his life; had rested upon His bosom, had witnessed His death, had talked with Him after His Resurrection. His eyes had seen, and his hands had handled, the Word of Life. YET WHEN HE SAW HIM GLORIFIED HE FELL AT HIS FEET AS DEAD!

Think on the incredibility of that! John could look with undimmed and undaunted eye on the Throne of Jasper, and behold the Gates of Pearl, gaze in wonder at the Crystal Sea, and even look upon the horrors of Hell, and still his soul did not tremble nor his spirit quake; but when he saw the great King in His beauty, and knew Him to be the glorified Son of Man, he fell as dead at His feet!

When John viewed the unimagined loveliness and undimmed holiness of Christ he became conscious of the burden of his own insignificance and iniquity. John had seen him AS HE IS! Into the forever of forever, He will evermore be the same. Always and only ALTOGETHER LOVELY!

Chapter Fourteen

WHERE FLOWERS NEVER FADE

Let it be thought incredible that anyone could be so insensitive to beauty as to not love flowers and gardens. It is said that Martin Luther always kept a flower on his desk for inspiration. My mother passed on to me a love of the pastoral. I suspect when I reach heaven it will be to find her inside the Eastern Gate walking among the flowers. "Just inside The Easter Gate" was her favorite song, and her dying words, whispered in my ear, were to not forget the flowers.

God is the Eternal Botanist. He has always enjoyed gardening. Little wonder Mary supposed the risen Lord to be a gardener (John 20:15). Way back in "the world that was", God cared for a garden. Then sin came and the loveliness of it all was ravaged. But when the chaotic world was remade, God started over with another garden called Eden, and placed man there with implicit command to keep it.

God enjoyed the delights of Eden so much that He came to walk in it in the cool of the evenings. Is anything more pleasant than that? Perhaps the fine feathered bird band played His favorite numbers at that time. Surely the hymn writer had this in mind when he wrote, "I come to the garden alone...", for he knew God would be found there.

God is so fond of gardens that he arranged for all the great pivotal events of world history to take place in a garden. The RUIN of man occurred in a garden (Gen 3:1,3). The REDEMPTION of man transpired in a garden (John 18:1). The RECONCILIATION of man came about in a garden (John 19:41, Rom 5:10). The RESURRECTION took place in a garden (John 19:41-42, 20:1,6). The RAPTURE will occur in a garden (Song of Solomon 4:12, 16). The RENEWED world will be a universal garden (Isa. 41:18-20). And surely the wedding RECEPTION of the Bride will be held in the Royal Gardens! The world began with Eden, and will end with Eden.

How thrilling to discover that God PLANTED a garden (Gen. 2:8). He did not assign the task to angels. He did it! Therefore how beautiful

Eden must have been in appearance and arrangement. Scholars tell us the world "planted" means transplanted. Apparently God transplanted some things from the heavenly gardens; things of special delight to Him intended for our enjoyment. What variety there must have been. Even now in the Holy Land there are some eighteen hundred known flowers.

If God "so loved the world", how beautiful this planet must have been. In the days of recreation it is recorded that God said three words after everything was made. Every day He looked upon His work and exclaimed, "It is good"! The connotation suggests that God took a seat in the bleachers like a spectator, and when He viewed what had been accomplished He arose, clapped His hands in delight, and shouted, "BEAUTIFUL! BEAUTIFUL!

The Bible is an Arboretum, a Divine Conservatory of exquisite beauty. All the hand of God touches is graced with regality and wonder, whether it be His Word or His Work. All God made reveals the impress of His finger, be it in miniature or magnitude. How delicately God designed the wing of the butterfly, tenderly placed the seraphic shine on a baby's velvet face, tossed a thousand blending colors into the sunset, touched the radiant rose with a tinted hue, pitched the song in the throat of the Warbler, and said "Sing". He weighed the mountains in scales, meted out the heavens with a span, and measured the waters in His hand. He caused the clouds to speak with thunder, the whirlwinds to perorate with screams, the cataracts to converse with roaring, but the flowers to convey His messages in a whisper.

Why the unfolding wonders of the Almighty parade before us in endless magnificence. We witness it all with a tear in our eye, for we know that sin broke a gaping hole in the wall of paradise and with it came the fall of man and the fading of the flowers.

However God has another garden untouched and unmarred by sin, where roses never fade. Never will it be infested with thorns and thistles. Never shall it know the curse. Thoughtless hands will not despoil it. Paul verifies such a garden exists for he was there. He was caught up into Paradise (II Cor. 12:4). The word for Paradise is literally, "The Royal Gardens"! It is the Utopia the world has dreamed of, but never found. Billows of color surge across the fields and up the hillsides. It is so lovely it is "unspeakable".

The festal flowers abloom in Paradise will ever remind us of our blessed Saviour. In fact He is pleased to be called by their names. He is the Rose of Sharon, the Lily of the Valleys, the Root, the Plant of Renown. In the greatest sermon ever preached in the Bible He spoke of the Lily. Our Lord was such a lover of flowers that He designated His burial place to be amid the floral fragrance of a garden (John 19:41-42).

Gardens are like lasting memorials. Remember when we walked with little ones in hand and watched with delight as they discovered pretty flowers. Even dandelions were precious to them. Lovers also seem to gravitate to the floral fairways. Memory perhaps holds a time when someone placed a flower in your hair, and the world seemed glittering with gladness, while your heart was held in the spell of happiness. So much is expressed with flowers. The Royal Gardens will hold sweet memories for us of loving trysts with our Lord. We will breathe the perfume of illimitable flowers, all an expression of His love for us.

The garden of God has foundations bejeweled with every precious stone, and the high amethystine walls are aromatic with climbing jasmine. The garden gates are of solid pearl, and the walkways of purest gold. It is so beautiful that John describes it as a bride adorned for her husband. That special day is one that holds something a husband never forgets. Years may come and go, gray hairs adorn the temples and intermingle with threads of gold, wrinkles grace the cheeks and brow, but never is forgotten the way she looked that day when adorned just for him. And we shall never forget Jesus, the fairest flower of them all.

How beautiful heaven must be. God is extravagant with beauty. Have you ever seen a sunset when clouds were burning with fire and there is gold, crimson, orange, blue, and a riot of rainbows in the sky? Is there one who can tell us any earthly reason for a sunset? They are not for sale, cannot be kept or put to use, nor accounted of any earthly value. What good are they? Just this, that God loves colors and things that are beautiful. He took the azure blue of the heavenly chalice, the surf of the raging sea, the emerald of the August sunset, and crystalized them all into living color to grace His gardens and flowers.

Everything shall remind us of the unsurpassing beauty and sweetness of Jesus. We shall respond as Solomon when he looked out of the palace windows upon the stately gardens spread below. As he breathed the fragrant aromas floating up to him, he was reminded of his lovely Lord, and cried out, "My beloved is unto me as a bed of spices, as sweet flowers"!

Our Lord shall forever be exquisitely the same. Though he changeth not, we shall find Him becoming more precious as the ages of eternity unfold. Like the flowers of paradise, His beauty will never fade away!

Chapter Fifteen

CLIMBING UP THE ROUGH SIDE

In the quietness of a motel room I turned on the television and watched a negro Gospel musical. It was such a blessing. Toward the end of the telecast they introduced an elderly gentleman, blacker than the darkness of midnight, whose crown of snow white hair lent him a silent dignity. His eyes held the faraway look of the distant seer. His wrinkled face spoke of the weathering of many storms. It radiated a heavenly glow as he sang.

Never before had I heard the song, and never before had a song gripped my heart as did this one. I found myself leaning closer to catch the words which cast a sweet spell upon me. He sang, "I'm Climbing Up The Rough Side Of The Mountain." And memory lends assurance that the song and chorus went something along this order...

"This old life will soon be done,
There'll be no more race to run;
And I'll stand before God's throne,
All my heartache will be gone.
And I'll hear Him say 'Well done, welcome home.'
    I'm climbing up the rough side of the mountain.
    I just hold to God's all-powerful hand.
    And as I go from day to day,
    I can hear my Saviour say,
    'Climb on my child, you're almost home.'"

This heart of mine was held in rapt agreement and I said, "I identify with you my brother." He had sung the same truth Paul preached to the churches when he exhorted them to continue in the faith, and that we MUST through much tribulation enter into the kingdom of God" (Acts 14:22). Suffering is one of the imperatives of the christian life. We must all climb the rough side. There are no exceptions.

Multitudes of the redeemed have sailed through bloody seas, countless have walked through furnaces heated seven fold, many were stoned, others sawn asunder, some wandered, destitute, afflicted, tormented, but they all went on in faith. Paul concluded the great chapter of faith by saying that "the world was not worthy of them", that they "wandered in MOUNTAINS", but they all reached the summit, for they all "obtained through faith" (Heb. 11:38-39).

Moses was a mountain climber. He forsook the wealth of Egypt because he had gotten a glimpse of the riches of Christ. His climb took him up the rough side of rugged Sinai. There, hidden in the cleft of the rock, he gazed on the afterglow of God and became the man with the shining face. It was well worth the climb, for Moses had seen HIM!

Abraham climbed the rough side. He saw the mount far away, fixed his eyes upon it, and began climbing, full well knowing that it meant the giving up of all earthly hopes and dreams in the sacrifice of his only son Isaac. But it was worth the climb for he saw Christ (John 8:56).

Caleb, the grand old man of the mountain, climbed the rough side fighting giants all the way. That senior saint with another spirit had the ascending vision. He was still climbing at the age of eighty-five! It was worth the climb for he saw Christ and gained Hebron (fellowship), and from that great height caught the gleams of the coming day.

John climbed the mountain while suffering the solitude of Patmos (Rev. 21:10). But it was worth the climb for he saw the Throne and the emerald rainbow round about. He looked upon the Lamb that was the Lion. He beheld the glass-like Crystal Sea, and the New Jerusalem with its jasper walls and river of life. He viewed the consumation of all things when he saw the King of Kings and Lord of Lords coming in great power and glory.

John, what can you tell us now that you have scaled the mountain? And John cups hands to mouth and shouts the encouraging words that have come in reverberating echoes down through the centuries...NO MORE NIGHT...NO MORE NEED...NO MORE SORROW...NO MORE CRYING...NO MORE PAIN...NO MORE DEATH...THE MORNING STAR IS APPEARING...AND WHEN YOU SEE HIM IT WILL BE WORTH IT ALL...KEEP CLIMBING...YOU ARE ALMOST HOME!

Keep on climbing child of God. The going will get rough at times, but it is worth the climb. Keep climbing for we are almost at the pinnacle. The crest is about to be reached. Sunrise is about to break over the top. Even now we feel the cool breezes of Beulah, and hear the singing and shouting of victory up ahead. Like Job our ash heap may seem as mammoth as Mount McKinley, but like Job you will be able to say, "Now mine eyes seeth HIM!"

Chapter Sixteen

MY LORD AND MY GOD!

Throughout my years of ministry. I have sought with a passion to read what others wrote about our lovely Lord. In sundry ways, such as in begging, borrowing, buying, or bestowment, I have gathered over fifty volumes by Charles Haddon Spurgeon, England's prince of preachers. After plumbing the depths with that literary leviathan I wondered if anything more exalting could be said by any preacher concerning Jesus Christ.

As a young pastor I attempted to barter a set of T. Dewitt Talmage from my wife's pastor. Of course it was to no avail for no pastor in his right mind would part with his books. That would be tantamount to forsaking your family! Wearying of me he finally said to his sister, "When I die give these books to Knauss." And he died a month later! But to read Talmage is to entertain eloquence. What oratorical overtures. While absorbing his words I sat like the young men before Job, with a hand over my mouth, and thought, "Surely nothing lovelier could be said about Jesus Christ!"

Robert G. Lee could draw a picture without ever putting hand to brush or canvass, and when I heard him preach on Christ I was persuaded he had delivered the entirety, that I had been caught up to paradise at the third heaven and was hearing the unspeakable words. Along with a multitude of others I have attempted to magnify the person of Christ, and felt as one standing by the ocean with the impossible task of dipping that ocean dry a handful at a time, and all the time that ocean growing larger and larger and my hands smaller and smaller. He is beyond compare, beyond description, His wealth inexhaustible and His worth inexpressible.

Reach back into yon years and bring forth the homage given Christ by others. Mortal tongue has ascribed Him in many ways, and we lend support with loud Amen's. Ask Isaac Watts, the hymn writer, "What is Jesus Christ to you?" And he pens the words, "When I survey the wondrous cross, on which the ...yes, call Him PRINCE OF GLORY! That is what He is to me."

Ask John Newton, the converted slave trader, what Jesus means to him, and Newton takes quill in hand to write the music of his heart, "Amazing grace, how sweet the sound...yes, call Him AMAZING GRACE!" Ask William Cowper, and he writes, "There is a fountain filled with blood, drawn from...yes, call Him EMMANUEL!" Put the same question to Fanny Crosby, the sainted blind lady, and she too answers in song, "When my life's work is ended and I cross the swelling tide, and the bright and glorious morning I shall see, I shall know my...yes, call him REDEEMER; that is what He is to me." And what would Charles Wesley say? He stands by an open window and as he meditates a bird flys into his vest to escape the storm, and he is inspired to write, "Jesus lover of my soul, let me to thy bosom fly...yes, call Him LOVER OF MY SOUL!"

Step beyond the age and into antiquity and listen to some higher testimonials. Solomon, how would you describe Him? And Solomon dips into his well of wisdom and says, "He is the LILY of the Valleys, the ROSE of Sharon, the CHIEFEST of ten thousands, the FAIREST OF THE FAIR, the ALTOGETHER LOVELY." And David, what is your response? With harp held to heart David begins to strum, and his soul breaks forth into song, "The Lord is my SHEPHERD!" Then out of the darkness of Patmos comes the voice of John crying, "He is the BRIGHT AND MORNING STAR!" But Paul outdoes them all. In the impoverishment of his prison cell he declares the satisfying summation, "Christ is ALL IN ALL!"

Who is there in love with Christ but what will sooner or later break forth into praise to Him! The Spirit of God hath impressed Him upon our memories. Can the slave forget who freed him? Can the blind forget who gave him sight? Can the prodigal forget who brought him home? Never! He is forever unforgettable! It will be the insignia borne on every flag, the title braced by every banner, the password breathed at every gate. The red horse of carnage, the pale horse of plague, and the black horse of death, will all fall back as the white horse of victory emerges through the open gate of heaven, mounted by Him whose vesture is dipped in blood and whose name is called THE WORD OF GOD!

We shall raise the windows of Paradise, breathe the fragrance of the eternal morning, and call Him BREATH OF HEAVEN. We shall gather in the King's gardens, all abloom with everlasting springtime, and call Him MY LILY, MY ROSE. We shall stroll along the river of life, with its clear waters cascading like silver chalices, and call Him MY FOUNTAIN. And when we walk through the green pastures of the hills of home we shall call Him, as did David, MY SHEPHERD. But when we look full in His wonderful face, and behold the wounds of His hands, and remember His grace that saved sinners the likes of us, we shall fall prostrate at His feet in wonder and worship, and cry "MY LORD AND MY GOD!"

Chapter Seventeen

AMEN AND AMEN!

The saying of "Amen" is an integral part of true worship. It is like breathing the precious name of Jesus. It means "so be it". When a solemn oath was pronounced by a priest the people responded with loud "Amen". In like manner when we hear the Word of God clearly set forth, and Christ uplifted, our hearts should also respond with "Amen".

The Old Testament has about thirty references to Amen. In the New Testament there are found fifty such references, In each instance it is the supportive word of affirmation and confirmation. It holds the force of finality. When one has said "Amen" there is nothing more to say. You cannot add to it! All you can do is repeat it, or double it. Of course if Amen is worth saying in the first place, it is worth repeating in the second place.

The congregation of Nehemiah kept the Amen Corner hot in that manner. When Nehemiah read and commented on the Scripture ALL the people cut loose with both barrels, "Amen, Amen" (Neh. 8:6). All of them! Even the timid ones! It was common for the Jews to say Amen in the synagogue, and once in a while we hear it gracing our services today. It was customary to say Amen at the giving of praise or prayer.

While the word "Amen" is found first said by women (Num. 5:22), it appears that Abraham was the father of it. God directed Abraham's attention to the heavens and promised that his seed would be as numberless as the stars, and Abraham BELIEVED God (Gen. 15:5-6). While we know that faith existed prior to this, here is the first time we read that a man "believed in the Lord"; and it is better translated, "and he said AMEN to the Lord."

Seraphims minister amid worshipful Amens (Isa. 6:1-3). Isaiah began his book informing us that when King Uzziah died he saw the Lord, and the all glorious throne was attended by Seraphims, the protectorate of God's holiness. They twain did cover their faces and feet with their wings because of unworthiness. The Seraphim on the north end of the Mercy Seat veiled his face and cried "Holy!" The Seraphim on the south end of the Mercy Seat could not improve on that so he cried "Holy!" Together they glorified the thrice Holy God, "HOLY, HOLY, HOLY!"

Amen and Amen!

There are no degrees of holiness with God. He is not more holy today than He was yesterday, nor will He be less holy tomorrow than He is today. He is always HOLY, HOLY, HOLY! We agree with that so we might as well say "so be it", or "AMEN!" Amen is another way of saying, "Lord, this is not the mere expression of my lips, it is the language of my heart." Amen is saying, "Yes, I am in agreement with God." Too few seem in agreement with God.

Heaven resounds with Amen, and the Revelation is the Book of the Grand Amen. We find the word "Amen" there more than in any other Book of the Bible. In fact the Book of Revelation closes with "Amen". Under Law it was the Curse, but under Grace it is the AMEN! Oh Amen and Amen!

The Greek equivalent to the Hebrew "Amen" is VERILY. Only in the Gospel of John is it ever found double, "Verily, Verily"". Our Lord used it tandem style twenty-four times to emphasize divine certainty, for each time a double "verily" is given it is followed by "I say unto you." For instance to Nicodemus He said, "Verily, verily...I say unto thee...ye must be born again." That leaves no doubt as to the necessity of the New Birth. Yet, if we are correct, the Lord spoke the word "Amen" only three times. Surely those three instances must hold special significance for us.

Consider the "Amen" of His Commissioning (Matt. 28:19-20). The first time our Lord said "Amen" was upon the commissioning and sending forth of the Apostolic Advance into the world to preach the saving Gospel of His Death, Burial, and Resurrection, and to baptize those who believed, and in turn teach those believers to observe the same things. And when He viewed that little regiment of redeemed going forth to engage the powers of wickedness, and to establish churches in enemy territory, He shouted, "Amen"! So be it!

The second instance provides the "Amen" of His Conquering (Rev. 1:18). John had just beheld for the first time his glorified Lord, and had fallen prostrate at His feet. Who would not! Then our Lord took the right hand of His omnipotence, laid it upon John, and said, "Fear not...I am He that liveth and was dead, and behold I am alive for evermore." And then He confirmed that immutable truth with "AMEN!"

Our Lord could look back on the Cross, see the empty Tomb with grave clothing lying untouched, see death robbed of its sting and the grave of its victory, see how He had triumphed over principalities and powers, blotting out the handwriting of ordinances against us, making a shew of them openly, and our all conquering Christ held high the wrested keys of Hell and Death and cried, "AMEN!"

Lastly we find the "Amen" of His Coming (Rev. 22:20). When our Lord spoke the final Amen it was after He had shown John the preview of His complete overthrow of wickedness, the judgement of satan and sinners, His coming in power and great glory with ten thousands of His saints, and the New Jerusalem descending out of heaven adorned as a Bride for her husband. Upon that blessed note He closed the volume of the Book with the last word of promise, "Surely, I come quickly." Then He shouted as the lordly Lion, loud in triumph, "AMEN!" And my heart shouts it too! So be it! Amen and Amen!

Chapter Eighteen

"ABIDE WITH ME"

Do you know that the first word about God in Scripture reveals something about His Power? "In the beginning God created the heaven and the earth" (Gen. 1:1). Do you know that the second word about God in Scripture reveals something about His Person? "And the Spirit moved..." (Gen 1:2). And did you know that this very first revelation about the person of God reveals Him in tears? God's lovely masterpiece of creation had just been reduced to ruin because of sin, and the Spirit WAS moved! Be sure to include the definite article "WAS". God cried! The Sovereign was sobbing!

When I was a small child I saw a man run across our yard to pick up his son just struck by a car. He carried the unconscious form in his arms, and cried! That is what John means when he says, "The whole world lieth in wickedness" (I John 5:19). It is better translated, He (the Holy Spirit) holds the world unconscious in His arms". Do you suppose He is still sobbing over this world?

How vivid then is this opening picture of Scripture. The world had just been run over by sin, and the Holy Spirit in touching tenderness gathered it up in His almighty arms and cried over His unconscious creation. Oh the infinite compassion of God!

Why should the Spirit cry? Surely He cried because sin had made chaos of His handywork. Furthermore He cried because it now meant that the predetermined plan of redemption must begin and the Son of God take upon Himself the form of sinful flesh and die. But my heart tells me He sobbed uncontrollably when He realized it meant He would be coming to live in the likes of us. And now you know the rest of the story. The Son of God came for our Salvation. He came to save our souls. But the rest of the story is that we have a second Saviour. The Holy Spirit came for our Service. He came to save our lives! Call Him your Saviour and Lord, if you will, for He came in the name of Jesus (Jh. 14:26). He came to be all to us that Jesus ever would be. He came that the world might see our lovely Lord in us.

When we receive Christ as our Savior, the Holy Spirit immediately

"Abide With Me"

---

makes His eternal residence in us (Jh. 14:16). Yet in a very real sense the entire Godhead comes and makes their home in us! Jesus said, "If a man love me, he will keep my words...and my Father will love him, and WE WILL COME UNTO HIM, AND MAKE OUR ABODE WITH HIM" (John 14:23). How incredible that all three persons of the Godhead should make their home in these temporary houses of clay.

Abraham loved God, and the more he knew God the less he was interested in this world and what it had to offer. God knew Abraham loved Him so the entire Trinity visited him and fulfilled this promise. It was at eventide, in the heat of the day, when three heavenly visitors arrived at Abraham's tent on the plains of Mamre (Gen. 18:1). It was "God in three Persons!" They came in a manner and form that Abraham could comprehend, and they lodged with him and they supped together. What a day!

In sharp contrast, when Lot received heavenly messengers only two came (Gen. 19:2)! Lot never did know the power of the Holy Spirit. He knew God in creation, and the Lord in redemption, but the reality of the Holy Spirit is unknown to the worldly christian.

Abraham however had separated from this world, and had no other Master but his Lord. There was nothing preoccupying his attention, and when the Lord appeared He ran to meet Him. The Holy Spirit upon Abraham drew him immediately to the Lord. Likewise, the Spirit of God within us is ever working to draw us to Christ and make us more like Him.

Few people seem to know and appreciate this wonderful Person called the Holy Spirit. Because of His ministry there is deep within every child of God a restlessness, a dissatisfaction with himself, a gnawing desire to be more like Christ; and if a believer does not have that longing there is something terribly wrong. The blessed Spirit creates within us that longing for Christ; to know Him, to know His Word, and to do His will.

How well do you know this precious Person? In all the years since you have been saved have you ever thanked Him for coming to live with you? Have you ever welcomed Him? Have you ever gotten acquainted with Him? Suppose you came to live with me at my invitation, slept in my rooms, dined at my table, sat on my sofa, and that went on year after year and not once did I ever converse with you, even to say, "I'm so glad you came to live with me!" How wanted would you feel? How wanted must the Holy Spirit feel?

Oh, that God might feel at home in this unworthy one. Abide with me, fast falls the eventide.

Chapter Nineteen

DEAD...YET!

Journeying through John is like steadily climbing a mountain in that each chapter brings one a little higher than the preceding one. And what a grand height is attained in the tenth chapter where is viewed the believer held securely in God's hand; and nothing ever able to pluck them out.

However in chapter eleven we read a strange thing. Strange because one whom the Lord loved appears to be snatched from His omnipotent hand. Suddenly death invades holy ground and Lazarus sickens and dies. Little did Lazarus know that death was to be his greatest blessing on earth! Lazarus is a man whose name is not known, nor voice heard, until the time of his death. Even then he speaks not, nor is it recorded that he spoke after being raised from the dead. He had lived with two sisters and perhaps learned to keep still. Or it may be he was just a quiet man who loved silence and obscurity. We call him the Silent Saint of the New Testament, yet no man spake in death so loudly as Lazarus.

His death gave occasion for the seventh miracle of John's Gospel, which also becomes the last and greatest miracle of our Lord. Of all the earthly works recorded of Christ, none so reveal His matchless character as this. While John's Gospel is written to set forth the Deity of Christ, this chapter shows forth His Humanity. He weeps deeply. He is touched by human feelings. He seeks direction to the tomb. He asks for help to roll away the stone. He prays. He mingles His tears with ours. He groans with our grief. He reveals the tenderness of His heart, the power of His voice, the limitations of His flesh, and the sympathy of His spirit. We find grief and gladness, tears and triumph, all blending to make this the crowning miracle and message.

Walk again amid the misery of Bethany. Lazarus is sick. Some would have us believe the child of God should never be sick. Lazarus could explain that sickness is not a sign that God does not love us. But sometimes circumstances do appear misleading, and seem to say otherwise. Despite Lazarus being dearly loved of our Lord, he was allowed to sicken and die. In fact our Lord failed to respond to the urgent call to come. He stayed away. Too often our minds tell us God is cold and calloused, and uncaring

Dead...Yet!

about what concerns us.

The sisters sent word, "He whom thou lovest is sick!" That should have brought our Lord on the run. But He did not come. In fact He remained where he was until Lazarus died! He did not so much as send a get well card, or sympathy note, or register His name at the funeral home, or attend the memorial service. At times it seems God just steps clear of our sorrow and sufferings; that He is never there when we need Him most.

Martha said, "Lord, if thou hadst been here my brother had not died." In other words she felt the Lord could have stopped it. And "even now" He could change it. How often we have looked on the suffering of loved ones and felt bitterness welling up within because it seemed God was not answering prayer, nor doing anything about the situation. Martha looked at the circumstances and was wrong in her conclusions. No one cared more for Lazarus than the Lord. It was that our Lord knew glory, not death, was the final issue.

However when Jesus finally came His comfort was measureless. He gave the sorrowing sisters two of the most astounding truths to ever dawn on human hearts, or grace our minds; two things which you and I need to settle once and for all..

First, THE DEAD SHALL LIVE! Jesus said, "He that believeth in me, though he were dead, yet shall he live" (John 11:25). Did you catch that? Grab ahold of that wonderful word YET! Our Lord did say the believer shall live again, but that he YET LIVES! Our Lord would have us to understand that any believer overtaken by death still lives! Dead...yet shall he live!" Despite all outward appearance, despite how things look, he LIVES!

The child of God never dies! There is no such thing as death to us, for we have passed from death unto life (John 5:24). David knew this to be true when he wrote, "Ye though I walk THROUGH the valley of the shadow of death..." Death could not stop him. Death was but a shadow, not a reality. Death is just part of the believer's journey, and he walks THROUGH it! Never say of the departed believer that they are dead. That would be to talk as a pagan talks. They are not dead! They are with the Lord. Now if you think that truth is incredible then ponder the other half.

THE LIVING SHALL NEVER DIE! Jesus went on to add, "And whosoever liveth and believeth in me shall never die" (John 11:26). Can you believe that! Never die! How do we dare say such a thing? Because our Lord said so! Your body may be temporarily laid away, but you shall never die!

62

You will not live again, for you shall keep on living. How can one live again if he never dies? "Yet shall he live!" We shall dwell in the House of the Lord forever!

When we laid the body of my lovely mother in the grave I thought my heart would tear asunder. Her pastor called upon me to say a word, and from deep within me rose a cry, "Don't ask me to do this!" But when I stood on her grave it suddenly dawned upon me what our Lord had said, and I knew she was not there. We had just honored he body. SHE HAD NEVER DIED; for believers never die. They live forever.

Someone interjects, "But Lazarus died!" Did he? Come, let us prove otherwise. Follow our Lord as He makes His way to the tomb. He lifts His eyes and prays, and then with a loud voice, so all can hear, says, "Lazarus, come forth!" Did He think the dead could not hear? But would you believe Lazarus heard Him, and came forth! HE WAS NOT DEAD AFTER ALL. Yet he lived!

The greatest thing that can happen to a child of God is to escape this world by way of death so he can get on with eternity. That is his victory! Paul wrote fourteen books of the New Testament and only used the word "VICTORY" three times; all found in a cluster (I Cor. 15:54-57). And would you believe Paul used that word only in the context of triumph over death. To Paul death was not tragedy, it was triumph.

Let the body lay in its grave to await the resurrection, for the tenant lives on. The child of God shall live on long after the stars have been pulled from their sockets of blue, long after the earth has burned to a cinder, long after the heavens have been folded up and cast away as an old garment. YET shall he live!

Chapter Twenty

Loneliness

Step with me into the portals of Psalm One Hundred Two and behold a picture of unparalled sorrow and suffering. Then lift verses six and seven from their setting and feel them pulsate with the pains of life and throb with the pangs of loneliness. The suffering psalmist is garbed in the sackcloth of solitude.

It is bad enough to suffer, but when the affliction of loneliness is added to suffering there is untold despair, and unimaginable agony. Loneliness is as universal as the common cold, and sooner or later everyone catches it. It is so common we tend to sweep it under the perverbial rug. But putting loneliness under cover will not make it disappear; for it is the most miserable millstone to be hung around the grieving spirit.

The British Broadcasting Company aired a program with an interviewer making this frightening observation, "Most people go through life in a COFFIN OF LONELINESS!" Had he fallen prey to exaggeration? Hardly! Life Line International analyzed millions of phone calls to one hundred thirty-two crisis counseling centers, in twelve countries, and found loneliness ranking with anxiety and depression as man's common problems.

Despair is the last emotional resort in the frail make-up of man. It is the surrender of mind and heart. It is somewhat of A DEATH IN LIFE. And the despair of loneliness defies all description because one cannot see an end to it, as they might when despairing of other things.

Yet it is in life's loneliness that we are taught so much about our Lord. For some reason God deemed it necessary that we learn what it is to be lonely. His life was fraught with loneliness. He was alone at birth; for the world received Him not. He was alone in the wilderness temptation. He was alone in Gethsemane, alone at Calvary, alone in Death. Even His Father forsook Him. He went through life and the winepress alone. He was so alone in life that He is described by Isaiah as a man of sorrows, and out of pity men hid their faces from Him.

To illustrate His loneliness the Psalmist uses the metaphor of the pelican which sits in solitude for hours with its head sunk down on its shoulders. The pelican is perhaps the most somber, austere bird. David said, "I am like a pelican of the wilderness...as a sparrow alone." Follow the wilderness waterways and observe the pelican's seeming life of isolation. Ever felt that alone? Our Lord did, and thus He understands your loneliness, and is touched by the feelings of your infirmities. He recognizes your touch when you feel after Him (Acts 17:27).

God knows the individual touch of His children. My father-in-law was on his death bed, and had no idea we were anywhere within miles. Arriving from a distant state we entered the hospital room to find him laying with his back toward us. My wife went up behind him and ran her fingers gently along the back of his neck, and he said, "I know that touch"! And God recognizes your touch when you reach out to Him.

There are many kinds of loneliness suffered by mankind. There is the Loneliness of Society, which the crippled man of John Five suffered. Our Lord was standing at the Sheep Gates alongside the pool Bethesda, and while watching the multitude waiting for the stirring of the waters, He noticed a man more needy than all, and asked, "Whilt thou be made whole?" His answer was the low cry of the lonely heart, "I have NO MAN!" For thirty-eight years he had been surrounded by a sea of humanity, yet suffered alone, no one to befriend or love him. Thus his suffering was multiplied.

Someone asked a man boarding a train where he was going. His response was, "I am going to see my kin in the mountains, it is too lonely in New York City." Like the little girl watching the coronation parade of Queen Elizabeth. Standing with the cheering thousands she viewed the horse drawn vehicle of state pass by displaying the monarch in the robes of regality, and said, "Mother, the Queen looks so lonely!"

How terrible to live in loneliness. In 1861 Charles Summer was nearly killed in a fight on the Senate floor. He recovered and was asked what he thought of most as he was on what seemed his deathbed. He replied, "I thought most that I had lived and was dying, and had never heard anyone say, I love you."

There is the pleasing loneliness of the ocean when only the breaking of the waves sound. There is the plaintive loneliness of the prairie when only the song of the meadowlark thwarts the silence. There is the picturesque loneliness of the mountains when only the sigh of the wind is heard through the forest. Yet there is a painful loneliness of Society, when one is elbowed by the throng yet feels no personal touch. The man at Bethesda's pool heard the sweet laughter of children, the steady hum of human activity, but had not one person to help him or to care. He was surrounded but alone. Then Jesus came.

There is also the Loneliness of Suffering, and Job could fill us in on that. The familiar saying is, "Laugh and the world laughs with you; cry and you cry alone." Job was so alone in suffering it seemed even God had forsaken him. And no suffering is so severe as when suffering alone. If you are coughing with tuberculosis it does not seem so bad if someone coughs with you. But it was through suffering alone that Job gained a glimpse of God, and could say, "Now mine eye seeth thee" (Job 42:5).

There is the Loneliness of Service. Any man who has labored in the service of God will say "Amen" to support the fact that ministering is often a lonely work. Pastors most always experience the loneliness of service, their wives being privy to the same feelings of forgottenness and friendlessness.

The Scripture sets forth many who served alone. Noah was a solitary voice in condemning a faithless world. Elijah, from the brook Cherith to bloody Carmel, knew aloneness. He served while the saints stood silent, and finally concluded he was the sole surviving saint. Paul had the experience of being lied about, and when the trial came no man stood with him. Stephen stood alone before an angry tribunal, knowing his death was the only item on the agenda. You may find this true as well.

However, though our Lord suffered loneliness as no other, He will not allow His own to ever be alone. His unfailing promise is, "I will never leave thee, nor forsake thee" (Hebrew 13:5). That blest promise holds through Disappointment, Debility, Distance, Divorce, Disease, Death. It covers all time. It embraces all territory. It includes all testing, trials, and trouble. It takes in old age. It holds true in times when loved ones pass away, when friends forsake us, and when sickness invades our lives. Whatever comes into this unfair life we can count on God's Presence in it all, His Peace through it all, and His Power for it all.

God, out of necessity, forsook His only Son; but has promised never to forsake you. "I will never leave thee nor forsake thee" (Heb. 13:5). "Lo., I am with you always" (Matt. 28:20). "He shall give you another Comforter, that He may abide with your FOREVER" (John 14:16). Be assured, child of God, you are never alone.

Chapter Twenty-One

THE CONSOLATIONS OF GOD

Job is believed to be the oldest Book of the Bible. Scholars agree it was written before Genesis or any other Book in Scripture; though they do not agree as to who wrote it. Its antiquity is accentuated by the fact that there is no mention of the Law, nor a Priest, or Prophet, and no mention of divine revelation. Still more amazing is the fact that Job should deal with the tests and trials of a child of God! It seems God wanted the first of the inspired writings to be concerned with the sufferings of a believer.

Think on that! God wrote a Book dealing with suffering and faith before He wrote the Gospel! He told us of a man in the land of Uz who lived by faith when he had no written revelation to support it.

In Job we find the child of God on his BACK...in Affliction.
In Psalms we find the child of God on his KNEES...in Adoration.
In Proverbs we find the child of God on his FEET...in Action.

Job is the story of how God made a good man better, and thus it becomes God's handkerchief to dry away our tears. The Bible compliments Job more than any other man. God said things about Job never said about Moses, David, Jeremiah, Paul, John, etc. The very first verse of his account is sufficient: "He feared God, hated evil, walked uprightly, and was perfect." Here was a man who pleased God by faith, yet right in the center of God's will HE FOUND HIS GREATEST AFFLICTIONS! Afflictions such as no one, outside of Jesus Christ, has ever suffered.

Despite Job's being spiritually mature he suffered the ultimate hurts. To pull aside the curtain on this drama of distress is to view unfolded a five fold test. The inspired penman said, "There was a day!" And those red letter days come to us all. This was the first of many such days for Job, and on this day he suffered the FINANCIAL TEST (1:14-17). It was the day of the big crash. Wall street was in shambles. Job lost all his possessions. And things always seem worse when the pocketbook is empty. Then came the FAMILY TEST (1:19, 2:9). He suffered the loss of his children. In one devastating blow all ten were killed! If you have ever suffered the loss of one child you might imagine what Job went through with the loss of ten. Added to that, though we are not certain, it appears this was too much for Job's wife and she forsook him. Matrimonial problems were brought on. After that came the FLESH TEST (2:7). Job suffered loss of the most precious possession. Health was removed. Upon that came the FAITH TEST (2:10). Job found himself trusting God when he could find no trace of Him. He was suffering without an explanation, but still believing. Finally came the FRIENDS TEST (2:11). This turned out to be the most trying of all, for it takes God forty more chapters to cover it!

It was these well meaning "friends", and we say that word with tongue in cheek, that added insult to suffering. However, while uttering things they did not understand, they did give some beautiful truths and suggestions. One of the rare gems they uncovered needs to be taken from the setting to better evaluate its worth. While Job had heaped upon him far more than mortal man ought to have, one of his comforters asked him this question, "Are the consolations of God small with thee?" (15:11)

The day came when God rebuked Job's miserable friends, and in turn doubled every blessing He had withdrawn from him. Once again Job knew health. Once again he sat in the gate to be looked upon as the greatest in land. Yet in the midst of sufferings came this one question which perhaps pierced his heart more than any other in the multitude of words, "Are the consolations of God small with thee?"

How do you look upon God's consolations? Are they small with thee? Are you suffering? Are you falsely accused? Is health failing? Is the cupboard bare? Has the family forsaken you? Are you weary in well doing, and wondering if living for God pays off? You are not alone, for the Class of Discouragement has many members. But Oh the consolations of God!

As a young pastor I became discouraged often. Fortunately God provided a neighboring pastor who always was willing to take time to counsel me. One day I went to his study to find encouragement and this brother, now eighty-five years old, told me this story. He had gone as a young man to South Dakota and for two years pastored a church, and from there he moved to Iowa to pastor. During the early years in Iowa the bottom literally fell out of everything for him. One of his sons was stricken with polio. The other was put down with rickets. To make things worse the doctors informed him his young wife was dying and there was no hope. Hospital and medical bills began to accumulate and he was unable to meet them. To top that off the church failed to pay the full promised salary.

With devastated heart he got alone to pray and said, "Lord, I quit! I'm done as a pastor. I am not giving up the christian life, and I am not done loving you, but I am done as your servant. You know I gave up a good business to serve you. You know I was raised an orphan and when I finally had a home and family of my own I gave them to you. You haven't been fair Lord. You haven't been square with me. I will never be able to pay this stack of bills. My family is sick, my wife is dying, and I quit!

The next day he went to a scheduled Gospel rally. About five hundred people were packed into the church. He arrived late and entered the auditorium just as a soloist was singing prior to the message. As my friend came through the door the soloist was launching into the chorus of the song, and the words he heard went something like this...

> "How sweet the voice of Jesus in my ear,
> You have not to fear...for I am with you here.
> And if through the storms of life you'll trust in me,
> I'll keep you on the firing line."

He said, "Brother Knauss, I walked right on past those five hundred people sitting there and knelt at the altar. I disrupted the meeting but I got my heart right with God."

Would you believe he went back home and found a pulpit committee waiting in his yard. He went to be the pastor of their church and had a ministry there of thirty-one years! Would you believe his two sons got well and both of them went into the ministry! Would you believe his wife, who was given up for dead, was still serving God with him when I knew him at age eighty-five! And would you believe that the nine doctors on her case, all cancelled their bills! Now you tell me, are the consolations of God small? Are they small with thee?

Chapter Twenty-Two

HIS STATUTES MY SONG

The Holy Spirit deemed it necessary to preserve for us a sweet segment of David's personal testimony: "Thy statutes have been my songs in the house of my pilgrimage" (Psalm119:54). That is the true confession of all who walk the way of Faith. And when the Holy Spirit moved Paul to pen the great Hallmark chapter of Faith, in Hebrews eleven, he supported that testimony by presenting a list of some sixteen Old Testament saints by name, and a number of others by inference.

They were all men and women with common faults and weaknesses. They staggered and fell beneath overwhelming burdens, but refused to stay down. They arose to keep traveling the Road of Faith knowing full well it would never get easier. It is recorded that they accepted the Inadmissible, believed the Incredible, gained the Imperishable, saw the Invisible, wrought the Impossible, and overcame the Intolerable; always keeping the promise of God in view (Heb. 11:39). It was their song when they could not sing.

Yet in that listing of Faith's Elite not every one is named. Search with magnifying glass and you will never locate Job! That pioneer Patriarch went on without revelation from God, but still believing! He is included with the host of faithful simply classified under the word "OTHERS"! Their victories are not mentioned. We are only told they suffered. They believed, but they did not escape. They wandered in faith, and found no deliverance (Heb. 11:36-37). They endured by seeing Him who is invisible, and His Word was their song.

The others believed that "the righteous cry, and the Lord heareth, and delivereth them out of all their troubles" (Psalm 34:17), yet God did not seem to hear nor deliver. They believed God but nevertheless were tried, scourged, imprisoned, stoned, sawn asunder, slain with the sword. Some wandered on, destitute, afflicted, tormented. How incredible to read, "BY FAITH...there were stoned...slain, etc. How do you account for this? Why is it some win the plaudits, and others suffer pain? Why do some prosper, while others live bedfellow with poverty? Most of us are among the

His Statutes My Songs

unnoticed and unheralded "others"; for faith that endures is far greater to God than faith that conquers.

It has not been my lot to witness God moving in marvelous, miraculous, mind boggling ways. I have not been called upon to be a Noah and alone withstand a wicked world, build an ark and see creation destroyed by universal flood. But I have found what it is to lie down in green pastures, and be led where living waters are springing up quietly, and not want.

It has not been my portion to be a Moses and lead God's people through Red Seas miraculously divided, over muddy ground instantly dried, or by way of deserts sustained daily, but I have found myself in tight corners, unable to turn right or left, and know what it is to be led out in plain paths.

It has not been my fortune to be an intellect like Paul, and astound the wise of this world with words and writings; but I have had the joy of preaching the unsearchable Word of God and seeing the spiritually dead rise to new life, and the hurting of heart awaken to faith and healing.

It has not been my part to be endowed with wisdom as was Solomon, or with eloquence as was Apollos, yet I have experienced the thrill of witnessing multitudes sit spellbound at the sheer beauty of God's Word as the Holy Spirit ministered.

I have not had the experience of Elijah in being caught up by fiery chariots, or in praying down rain or fire from heaven. Earth shaking, mountain moving, sea opening, heaven viewing miracles I have not known, yet God has mercifully inclined His ear to me and heard my voice.

The invisible God has never manifested Himself to me as He did to Abraham on the Plains, nor has He come to me as He did to Jacob at Peniel, or to John on Patmos, yet I have been in His presence, and He has deigned to walk with me and talk with me and call me His own.

It was not given me to be a David, and slay giant Goliaths, or hear the cheers of ten thousands as a King ascending his throne. But I know the feeling of David's heart when he said, "Thy statutes have been my song!" Like David and Paul I have been to that place where no man knew me, all men forsaking me, and discovered "nevertheless the Lord stood with me", that He never forsaketh His own.

I have not been called upon to go through deep waters, or enter fiery furnaces, or be thrown into lions' dens, or wander in deserts or mountains. Still, by His infinite grace, I know what it is to be lifted from the miry clay, have the shackles of sin broken, be washed whiter then snow, and know His blood has gone deeper than the stain has gone.

I have dreamed many dreams that have never come true, but I have realized enough of my dreams to make me dream on. I have prayed when no answer came, but I have had enough answers to prayer to make me pray on. I have sown much seed that fell on hard ground, but I have had enough sheaves in my hands to make me sow on. I have drained the cup of disappointment, but I have tasted enough nectar from the heather of the hills to make me want to live on. I have prayed when I could not pray, and sang when I could not sing, and kept on when I could not go on, for "His statutes have been my songs."

It has been my privilege to experience cupboards bare, and feel the ground through my shoes, and yet in that poverty find myself the object of His care; more precious than sparrows that fall or lilies that toil not. God has not seen fit to speak audibly with me, nor verify my faith and ministry with attending spectacular evidences. Still He has proven over and over that He is my God, my Friend who abideth faithful, and that His never failing promises are yea and amen.

I have walked in the darkness of the Valley of Shadow, and though I heard not the sound of His voice or footstep I was assured He was with me. Like the Prodigal Son I have had my feet in the filth of the Far Country, and came to abhor myself, and found grace greater than all my sin, and knew the tearful joy of hearing Him say, "Thy sins be forgiven thee." I know what it is to feel His Loving arms about me, hear music from home, see the table spread, and smell the roasting of the fatted calf.

I have stood among the broken hearted, shared grief at gravesides, felt tears unbidden flow, and God did not come to me as He did to Mary and Martha, or the widow of Nain. But I remembered His words, "He that believeth in Me, though he were dead, yet shall he live" and, "I will never leave thee nor forsake thee." Sorrowing I walked away, but with hope aglow in my heart, and kept going on in the way of faith...for His statutes were my songs!

Chapter Twenty-Three

JUST FOR THE RECORD

This old world has always had its crisis times. They came and passed along. But Paul wrote centuries ago that the end of this age would experience the coming of perilous times which would not pass by. He meant that perilous times would SET IN, like a storm without an end in sight. A blind man could tell that those times have arrived, for the world has gone crazy with rebellion and revolt against God. Man is in mutiny against his Maker.

Nothing is as it used to be. The righteous are witnessing the very foundations being destroyed. Listen closely and you hear the grating noises of anchors shifting as the tides of time move against those foundations. The waves are eroding the shore lines. The storms are battering the bulwarks. One authority made this startling observation, "America is dangling at the end of a rope of sand". He meant there is nothing solid to hold onto. The adhesiveness is gone.

Times have changed. Standards have changed. The mind of a man has changed. Patriots are belittled, cowards are glorified, traitors honored, and the welfare state encouraged. We are besieged with Punk, Pot, Pornography, and Pandemonium. We still are in the rat race, but a stranger and swifter breed of rats has come on the scene. We live in a hurried society. No one takes time to rest, get alone, or be quiet anymore. Meditation is a thing of the past. If you see someone out walking by themselves you assume they are either out of gas or out of their head.

Music has made a complete revolution. Remember the days when you could understand the words being sung ? There was a time when music made you tap your foot on the floor, now it makes you bang your head against the wall. This decadent generation has no conception of what worship is. The erosion of both music and message throughout christendom is embarrassingly evident. Self styled servants of God blast forth with a deafening instrumental and vocal tumult that can only be accurately recorded by a seismograph. All spiritual message is aborted as the performers take their cue from Hollywood and jive for Jesus. Shades of Pentecost!

Morals also have become unrecognizable. Sin no longer is exceedingly sinful. The world is rewriting the dictionary to do away with sin and guilt.

Just for the Record

Immorality has been given a face lift, and bears names designed to proffer self respect. Sin comes disguised in alluring garments. We are being educated to believe that wrong is right. Lust is now perceived as love. Adultery is placed under the classification of "situation ethics". Homosexuals are no longer sodomites, but "gays"; and sodomy is "sex preference". Abortion is not murder, but "choice"; the expression of human right! Illicit sex is "live in love'" and alcoholism is just an illness. The new demonically inspired theology makes sin nothing less than an exercise of human right, the doing of your own thing.

Is it any wonder that I get to thinking it would have been nice to have lived in another time? Especially in the earlier days of the Age of Grace. God has always had His great moments, and great men to go along with them. Holy men of God have come walking bowed beneath the immeasurable weight of the Divine Word and a Demanding Work. They have come treading through the tumult of their times, the voice of One crying in the wilderness. They have been declared the offscouring of a world unworthy of them while pointing men to the One worthy, the Lamb of God.

This mind envisions seeing some of those men, and living in their time. Oh to have been somewhere nearby on Mar's Hill to hear Paul confound the wise of that day with the Word of God, and put humanistic thinking in disarray. Or to have seen that man called Martin Luther, whose words were as fiery swords, who trod the field of his age like an armoured giant, the sound of whose footfall was heard in Rome, and made popes tremble. He marched on like an army with banners. What courage he displayed to nail his ninety-five theses on the church door at Wittenberg and thereby give birth to the Protestant Reformation. I would love to have watched his face and sensed his emotion when he stood before Church and State and refused to recant, saying, "On my conscious and the Word of God, I cannot"!

Imagine living in the memorable days of that trio of flaming Methodist evangelists, John and Charles Wesley and George Whitefield. Barred from ministering in the cold formal state churches of England, they took to preaching in open fields. Out of curiosity thousands assembled to stand and watch those firebrands burn; but England turned back to God. Imagine also trying to find a seat in the packed auditorium of London's Metropolitan Tabernacle, and hearing that immovable Baptist separatist, the unschooled Prince of Preachers, Charles Haddon Spurgeon, as he held men spellbound by sheer exposition of the Scriptures.

How exciting it would have been to witness the awesome Spirit-filled ministry of Charles Finney. The very presence of that Presbyterian, with the burning heart and eyes, seemed to produce unequalled conviction of sin, and prompt unimagined moving of the Holy Spirit in revival. He alone may have well changed the course of American history.

This heart would love to have experienced some of the brush arbor meetings of Peter Cartwright, the man from the hills who preached in a long snapping split-tailed coat. It is said that his preaching was so fraught with the power of God that sinners fell right and left as though felled by spreading cannon shrapnel.

Time will not permit to dwell on such worthies as D.L. Moody, Billy Sunday, etc. It was Moody who said, "The world has yet to see what God can do with that man who is completely filled with the Holy Spirit"; and he determined to be that man. Such men are stronger than all enemy armies put together. Such men are not politicians who "run" for something, but men of purity who "stand" for something. God has always had His men who stood against this corrupt world and preached a "Thus saith the Lord"! We need such an army today.

Tell me, is there not a gnawing desire in your heart, a deep down longing to see God move again as He has in times past? Oh for those days when the Spirit of God listed upon us and we wore the halo of heaven and witnessed genuine repentance of sin, and genuine revival.

Though I would love to have lived in some other times and experienced some of those glorious moments in history and revival, I confess to being most thrilled at living in this most momentous time of all, terrible as it is, for we are living on the threshold of the coming Christ! I am looking for His coming with tip-toe expectancy! That will be THE moment of all time! Think of the great privilege of being alive and remaining to witness the Rapture of the Church, and the gathering together unto the One who loved us and gave Himself for us.

Let us not be discouraged about the times, rather let us rejoice that THE TIME HAS ARRIVED! We are almost done with sin and this cursed world.

Chapter Twenty-Four

"NOW...BUT...THEN"

The common lot of believers seems to be that at times we all succumb to despair. Incredible as it sounds, Paul confessed to being cast down. "Nevertheless God, that comforteth those that are cast down, comforted us..." (II Cor. 7:6). Even saintly Paul got to the place where he needed help and comfort. Those times come to us all.

Paul reached the place of "Nevertheless God". There is nothing one needs to know half as much as the "Nevertheless God"! There will come many times and many things in life when that will be all you have left to hang on to. Problems, troubles, and sorrows will rapidly multiply. In the small hours of the night, when sleep has become a deserter, there will not be one thing on earth left to you but "Nevertheless God". And many times you will feel your situation has gone beyond that.

There was such a time in my ministry when I despaired to go on. All seemed hopeless. It appeared the sun had set and the end had come. The Little Flower and I sought to take a few days of quiet and motored to another state. While browsing through a store in a little village it so happened I chanced to meet an older brother in the Lord. Long ago age had forced him into retirement, and he was slow as he walked along. The face was lined, the eyes squinted, but I recognized him and gave glad greeting. I spoke his name and asked how things were. He paused a moment to register my voice and place me in his memory, then said, "Why Brother Knauss! The anchor still holds!"

From the soles of my feet to the crown of my head I could feel joy welling up within me. I wanted to run outside and shout to the world, "Did you hear that? THE ANCHOR STILL HOLDS!" My soul had gripped the truth that though the storms rage, and the deeps surge, the anchor ever holds. The storm had just overtaken me and blotted out my vision. I had become occupied with looking at the NOW of things instead of the THEN. That timely truth meant so much to me that to this day I sign most of my correspondence with , "The Anchor Still Holds". And the anchor holds because it is hooked firmly into the "Nevertheless God".

Salvation does not exempt us from trial and troubles. Often trouble arise

"Now...But...Then"

not of our own making. Some sorrows come to try us, and make us better. Often we cannot understand why. A case in point is Joseph. He was loved of his father and hated by his brethren. Sometimes that is all it takes to have the brethren hate you...just enjoy a little more success then they do. Recall how they took Joseph, placed him in a pit, sold him as a slave, and after many things he finally wound up in the slammer in Egypt. Hold it! The story does not end there. "BUT GOD meant it for good" (Gen. 50:20). Joseph could now say that for he had seen the design on the upper side of the tapestry. He knew the THEN of things.

Perhaps that night, feeling totally rejected, Joseph sat in the pit and cried, "Why?" When sold as a slave in Egypt he cried "Why?" In Potiphar's cold prison he cried "Why?" Joseph was looking through glasses darkly. He could see no rhyme or reason in anything. When falsely accused the glasses became darker, but through it all there was the whisper of God, "Fear not Joseph, for I am with thee; someday you will understand. Not NOW...but THEN."

Daniel lived in a day comparable to ours. Babylon was in confusion. The king in distress. Wise men were at wit's end. No one knew the answer. However God revealed to Daniel what was beyond the present. Therefore when he stood before the pagan king and court Daniel could boldly say, "I know you do not know why things are as they are. But God in heaven revealeth secrets, and maketh known what shall be..."(Dan. 2:28).

Daniel's God is our God. Present and coming world problems may be beyond understanding. We may not know what the future holds, but we know who holds the future. Today men's heart are failing them for fear as they witness the universal upheavals. And if we look at this NOW our glasses steam up, the vision becomes blurred. But God hath revealed to us what will be beyond this cursed NOW. We look to the coming THEN and see a Rapture, an Armageddon, a Great White Throne judgement, a Pearly White City, and Tears forever wiped away. The world is a mess, BUT GOD! Wickedness may appear to triumph, BUT GOD! We must look beyond the NOW to God's THEN.

We do see through a glass darkly, NOT THROUGH DARK GLASSES! It means our vision is dimmed. The present picture is not clear to us. Indeed we are hard pressed for explanations. But all we need to hold onto by faith is the truth contained in those three words, "NOW...BUT...THEN". We shall understand the reason for all things THEN. Let sickness come, let old age overcome, let sorrows roll on like a flood, let all hell conspire against us now, our THEN is coming.

Wait until the shadows lengthen. Wait until the blackness of night settles in. Wait until the cupboard is empty. Wait until the little feet are shoeless. Wait until friends forsake. Wait for the poisoned daggar to pierce the back. Wait until the furnace is heated seven times hotter. Wait until the grave becomes our blanket. Wait, for then we shall know! We shall see Him face to face! The miserable NOW will be swallowed up in God's merciful THEN.

Then we shall know the reason why the flaming chariots of God were permitted to roll their bloody rimmed wheels on heated axles through our lives, leaving their smoking desolating tracks along the way. Then we shall know why our loved ones were smitten down by death. Then we shall know why there was suffering and sickness and sorrow. Then we shall know the reason for bereavements and heartaches. God Himself will tell us. Or sainted loved one may lead us by the hand to flowered arbors along the river which maketh glad the city of God, and there explain God's mind to us in measures set to music, a thousand angels responding; and in thankfulness we shall rush to the foot of the Throne of Grace and pour out our gratitude for Why and How God chose to do as He did in performing that which concerned us.

When I was a boy we often sang a little chorus that still rings in my memory. In went something like this: "Cheer up ye saints of God, there's nothing to worry about. Nothing to make you feel afraid, nothing to make you doubt. Remember Jesus never fails so why not trust Him and shout..."YOU'LL BE SORRY YOU WORRIED AT ALL TOMORROW MORNING!"

Not NOW...but THEN!

Chapter Twenty-Five

NO MORE!

When Paul wrote the epistle to the Romans he gave us the Book of "MUCH MORE", but when John wrote the Revelation he gave us the Book of "NO MORE". John stood on the other side of time and pointed out ten specific things he discovered had passed away. Ten in Biblical numerics suggests legal perfection, as in the Law, and thus the government of God has settled the matter and stands behind the "no more".

John had just witnessed, in vision, the consummation of the ages. He had observed the doom of Babylon, the bloody battle of Armageddon, the seizure of satan, the Great White Throne Judgement, the sea giving up its dead, and death, with hell and the lost, being cast into the Lake of Fire. What relief must have swept across his troubled soul when God turned his eyes to behold the new heaven and new earth (Rev. 21:1,4). Scale the giant jasper wall, peer with John into the new Jerusalem, and rejoice because of some present heartaches which will be no more.

"NO MORE SEA!" Surely John wrote those words out loud! He must have shouted them while his pen was moving. The beloved disciple was about to describe the Land of Never Again, and the first thing to impress his mind was the fact that there was no more sea.

There is something INDEFINABLE about the sea. It represents mystery, death, unrest, evil. It is never quiet even when it is calm. But whether tranquil or turbulent the sea never fails to fascinate and lure the human heart. Who has not dreamed of setting sail to foreign ports? Yet every sea voyage recounted in Scripture met with shipwreck. When man sinned in Eden he was set adrift, and were it not for Him who comes walking on the waters where would this man be?

Rejoice, for in heaven there will be no more sea! There will be no more storm, no more shipwreck, no more sinking, no more separation. There will be no possibility of ruined vessels and wrecked lives; no more ventures, and no more failures. The aged apostle sat imprisoned on lonely Patmos and looked out upon the vast sea. It was an uncrossable barrier between himself and home. How comforting to him that soon the sea would be forever done away. The sea with all its unpredictableness, its often violence, would be gone, and in its stead an eternal calm.

"GOD SHALL WIPE AWAY ALL TEARS!" This was the second unique feature of the new earth that captivated John. The history of the world may be written down in one word, "Tears". Tears! Rivers of tears! In this cursed vale of tears all we seem to do is cry. It has been said that if every person shed but fifty tears a year, in a world of two billion people that would accumulate into forty thousand barrels of tears of tears per year; enough to float a battleship. But God shall wipe away all tears from our eyes; like a mother halts the hurt of her child, and then ministers comfort.

"NO MORE DEATH!" John said God would wipe all tears from our eyes, but Isaiah said that when death is swallowed up in victory God would wipe all tears from our FACES (Isa. 25:8). For the present we are harassed by death. There comes a time in life when we clasp hands for the last time, embrace for the final moment, look into the eyes for a closing recognition. Death inflicts wounds that time cannot heal. The casket with the body may be nearby for a few days, then it is removed. Days pass, the song is ended but the melody lingers. You feel you have gotten control of yourself, that the emotions are conquered, then suddenly a little shoe shows up, a book is opened and a golden lock of hair falls out, or a picture is uncovered, and the wound reopens and tears flow freely once more. But in our heavenly homeland there will be no crepe, no caskets, no crying, no curse; for death will be done away forever. It shall be "no more!"

"NO MORE SORROW!" Earth is thrust through with sorrow. Place your dreams alongside your disillusionments and find it true. Perhaps your road is ever uphill, and you find yourself always running against the wind. Children have not turned out as expected. Absolom has trodden hard on the heart. Your lot has been reversals of life; your bedfellows the twins of poverty and persecution. Take heart, there will be no disappointment in heaven. The history of broken hearts has now had its final chapter written. Go ahead, shout it. "No morrow sorrow!"

"NO MORE PAIN!" Let the afflicted one give praise. Beyond physical pain there will be no mental pain, no pain of poverty, no pain of shame, no pain of weariness. The hurting heart will ache no more!

"FOR FORMER THINGS ARE PASSED AWAY!" Death is gone, sorrow is gone, crying is gone, need is gone, night is gone, every plague of the present is wrapped up in those wonderful words, "the former things are passed away". All the miseries we see and experience now, all the memories we cannot blot out of mind, all are passed away. Not only will the old heaven and earth pass away, but every former nemesis along with them. NO MORE! NO MORE!

Chapter Twenty-Six

BEYOND THE TIDES OF TIME

Please journey with me back to the Edge of Eternity. Now let us join hands and step off into space. As we take the imaginary step we find ourselves moving in a trajectory before all things. Time is not yet known. We are proceeding out into the vast immeasurable expanses of eternity. How awesome is the limitless and timelessness of God. He is from "everlasting to everlasting"; as far as you can go both ways forever! No mater how far we traverse, or how long we search, we would never find the beginning of God.

"In the beginning was the Word, and the Word was God"! John means that when the beginning began GOD WAS THERE! He is Jehovah-Shammah (Ezekiel 48:35), "the God Who is THERE"! He was always there. He is still there for you!

Grope back to the furthest outposts of thought, where imagination touches the far side of pre-creation, and you will discover God THERE! He always WAS for He always IS. There is no beginning with God. There is that atheistic philosophy, that has shuttled so many to hell, that says everything that IS had to have a beginning. True, all things do have a beginning except GOD. GOD IS! And we must believe HE IS. When things began, God was already there.

You say, "but what about Genesis 1:1, where it says, 'In the beginning God'?" Well, the Bible does not say that. It says, "In the beginning, God CREATED"! It does not mean that God began, but that God was already there when things began. God had no beginning, for by Him were all things made, and without Him was not anything made that was made (John 1:3). God did not make Himself. HE ALWAYS WAS! He is God!

What went on back there at the beginning? Only God knows, because only God was there. Like the little boy who started off to school one day and on the way captured a bumble bee. He placed it in a bottle, put a cork on it, stuck it in his back pocket, and went to school. While in school he get to moving around in his seat and when the cork worked its way out of the bottle, business picked up downtown! The little fellow was wiggling this way and that, and the teacher finally said, "Johnny, why couldn't you sit still?" Johnny said, "Teacher, there was something going on back there that you don't know anything about!" And what went on back there in Eternity past we know nothing about. Only God knows for only God was there.

In the beginning God created the heavens and the earth, and then followed the parenthesis in Forever which we know as TIME. Between Eternity past and Eternity future flows the tides of the Ocean of Time. Those tides shall flow unabated until the mighty angel shall plant His feet on both land and sea, lift His hand heavenward, and swear by Him that liveth forever and ever, that time shall be no more.

God took the continuum of Time and divided it into Years (years add up to Decades, and Decades accumulate into Centuries, and Centuries arrange in Millenniums). God then divided Years into Months, and Weeks, and Days and Hours, and Minutes and Moments.

And there is a special moment that God has had His eye on, and which those who trust in Him have been anticipating. There is coming a moment, an infinitesimal split second of time, when every man in Christ Jesus will be raised out of the world DEAD OR ALIVE! In that brief span every child of God shall be changed (I Cor. 15:52-52).

Ponder that verse a moment. Not all of us will be dead when Christ comes. Some of us will be alive and remain. The A-Bomb is not going to destroy the world and you with it. Instead our Lord is coming to take us away. The trumpet will sound, the voice of the archangel will be heard, and we shall be changed...IN A MOMENT! That moment is so brief it is called the TWINKLING of an eye (not winking). So quickly shall we be changed and made immortal.

That magical moment shall make all other moments fade into insignificance and seem as nothing. This moment will outshine all other moments of time put together. It is THE moment for which our hearts have longed and waited and prayed for. It is "THE" moment! It is THE moment when we step out of the vale of tears and place our feet on Immanuel's shores.

We are out of time, and so it the world. When God made man He gave him dominion over the earth and all that is therein, but man was never given dominion over time! Time is in the hands of God. Therefore we need to trust Him while we have time allotted us. It is time to seek the Lord. Now is the accepted time. Today is the day of salvation. Get ready for we are standing on the step of Tomorrow!

Chapter Twenty-Seven

ETERNITY

O Eternity! All languages beg to express that word. When used in connection with the prospects of the Redeemed it is delightful; but when used in regards to the punishment of the wicked it is dreadful.

Eternity beggars description, it defies definition It has no past, no future, no ending, no beginning. It is older than the world, older than the heavens, older than the angels. It is as old as God, yet it is no older now than when all things were made, and never will it be any older, yet never was it any younger.

Eternity is the parent of the ages, coequal with God; the only type of Deity. Therefore what must its significance be when joined to the awful unending penalty of sin? From the lips of our lovely Lord came these words setting the extremes of Eternity. "These shall go away into EVERLASTING punishment; but the righteous into life ETERNAL!" He further described the asylum of the damned as a place of "UTTERMOST darkness! A place so far removed that it is like some Siberia of space, a region where light never reaches or penetrates; yet all the while it remains an unquenchable Lake of Fire and bubbling brimstone. Its' molten waves lash the ragged shorelines and its' flames lick every fissure and corner, while the fumes and smoke ascend and the everlasting lightnings flash and cross and beat time to the ceaseless groans of the lost.

Do you hold God's Word in question that there can be fire with darkness? Science has long ago discovered that the removal of ether from air will allow fire to burn unseen! Oh the everlasting misery of that man who lived his life without thought of God and Eternity, who refused to trust the Christ who came and died to save him from it all.

The punishment of the lost man is eternal because his penalty is reckoned in proportion to his guilt! If man's obligation to obey God is infinite, the guilt of disobeying God is infinite, and therefore the penalty, as a matter of right, is infinite.

That men are lost is beyond argument. Our Lord Himself said, "For the Son of Man is come to seek and to save that which is LOST" (Luke 19:10).

Eternity

Lost is a Scriptural word. Justice requires punishment for sin, as all admit, and the Bible says that wicked men and angels shall be tormented day and night, FOREVER AND EVER! That is righteous judgment. There is no annihilation, but there is everlasting retribution!

Imagine being lost forever in a world of burning darkness. Imagine being flung by the omnipotent hand of God out beyond creation's boundaries into immeasurable wastes of night, where no other world rolls into sight, no ray of light ever pencils an encouraging image, and where is no sound of children laughing and singing. Imagine being isolated from loved ones and friends, doomed to wail and wander alone while cycles roll and ages go grinding on. Oh the spirits of the lost, blackened with the curse of God, repeating in despairing cry the chorus of their eternal death-march, "LOST, LOST!" Lost in boundless, bottomless, infinite darkness, never to find company until the ghost of eternity greets them over the grave of God, and never resting until able to fold their weary wings on the gravestone of their Maker...and of that there is no possibility!

O Eternity! Lost men and fallen angels will be absorbed by thee when they are driven from the Judgment Seat and hear the ponderous gates of Hell closing behind them, and know the key of the gate is fastened to the girdle of God, and Divine Omnipotence is installed as perpetual sentinel to guard it.

O Eternity! Let thy ages tramp on, thy cycles roll. Thou art unable to crumble the charred walls of Hell, or rust and break its locks, or silver the hair of God who has sworn by His eternal Self that "the soul that sinneth shall surely die!" The pendulum over the gates of woe vibrates throughout the aeons, methodically repeating, "Forever, and Ever" - "Forever, and Ever", as its sounding bell strikes off the centuries and the ages.

O Eternity! God has wound up thy clock and it will never run down, and its tickings and beatings are heard by all the lost, "Forever, and Ever"- "Forever and Ever"!

"The wages of sin is death, BUT the gift of God is eternal Life" (Rom. 6:23). Death is reversible! John says, "He that hath the Son hath life, and he that hath not the Son, hath not life" (John 5:12). With Christ you LIVE FOREVER; without Him you PERISH FOREVER. It is that simple. Trust the sweet Son of God now and enjoy ETERNITY with Him!

Chapter Twenty-Eight

WINDSWEPT

Did you know the Bureau Standards in Washington claims that a dense fog covering seven city blocks to a depth of one hundred feet is composed of less than one glass of water? The amount of water is divided into about sixty billion tiny droplets. Yet when those minute particles settle over a city, or countryside, they can virtually blot out everything in sight.

Many live in such a dense fog today. They allow a cup of trouble to cloud their vision and change their course. You will agree it takes but little trouble to darken our world and dampen our spirit.

Trouble is something every man is born unto (Job 5:7), and the longer we live the better acquainted we become with it. Trouble sticks to us like glue. We cannot shake it off. We seem able to get rid of one trouble, then another strikes us. We get one bill paid and two more take its place. We often feel like Job who took a post graduate course in Affliction. With his boils alone he had more trouble than a one-armed paper hanger with hives!

But like it or not, trouble is our inheritance. And the very moment one enters this world they immediately set sail on troubled waters. Little wonder life is often compared to a voyage over turbulent seas. All depends upon how we set the sails of our soul in determining how our ship survives the storms, and if safe harbor is reached.

In the twenty-seventh chapter of Acts we find Luke's account of an incident often overlooked. It comes from the ship's Log Book, and is an historical account of Paul's last missionary journey. It provides the prime example of what we should do when skies darken, storms overtake, and our ship is about to go under.

The Log's first record says, "The south wind blew softly" (27:13). Now that is the way we like it! Oh those soft southern winds, the Floridian balm, that good feeling when all is going well. How sweet if the times are gentle on us. But weather, like other things, has a way of suddenly changing.

Thus in the next verse we find, "There arose a tempestuous wind". Luke called it a "Euroclydon", which is another way of saying, "a Northeaster"! The soft southern wind changed into a sweeping savage nightmare; and with it came days of devastating trouble.

"And the ship was CAUGHT" (vs 15). The mariners had not counted on this storm, nor had they taken heed of warnings (vs10). How true of us. A day may be ever so lovely, but we know not what it may bring forth. Suddenly the whole picture may change with a storm coming out of nowhere, and we find ourselves caught! WE BECOME A WINDSWEPT CHILD OF GOD! And often we are driven to blessing!

What should we do when trouble comes? Should we let it defeat us? Should we throw in the towel, lower the sails and just drift? Or should we overcome the adversity, and use it as a stepping stone of Grace?

There comes those moments in life when we need to check the sails, then wait on God. And often the hardest lesson to learn is to keep still and wait on God when we cannot see through the storm, when we are just windswept.

Isaiah put it sweetly, "But they that wait upon the Lord shall renew their strength, they shall mount up with wings as eagles; they shall run and not be weary; and they shall walk and not faint" (isa. 40:31). There is flying, for visibility. Running, for intensity. Walking, for consistency. But whatever aspect of life is being experienced, it is the waiting on God that counts. God has provided a way for us to see through the storm, and a way to keep on sailing.

When trouble comes life seems to stand still. Storms halt progress. It appeared to Paul that he might never reach Rome, for they SAILED SLOWLY MANY DAYS (vs 7). Paul was on a voyage that was part of the purpose and plan of God (23:11). Yet even on this divinely planned journey he SAILED SLOWLY many days. Oh the contrary winds God allows to teach us patience.

Often our highest and holiest desires are realized only after long waiting. We know we are moving in the direction of God's will, but oh so slowly. We fret and become restless. We are anxious to "get there". Yet the Unhurried God moves us steadily on across the sea of His Purpose, and in His own time we come to our Rome...on schedule. It is the set of the soul that counts.

Daniel was one of the few men of whom only good is recorded in the Scriptures. He was the beloved prophet, as John was later the beloved apostle. Three outstanding things produced the set of Daniel's soul; his Purpose of heart, Purity of Life, and Perseverance in prayer.

Daniel stood like an oak through the storms of life. He could not avoid the bitter blasts of Babylon, but he could purpose in his heart to not defile himself, and not act contrary to the will of God. Daniel determined to be true to God whatever the cost or consequence. Thus it is recorded, "Daniel PURPOSED in his heart...and Daniel CONTINUED" (Dan 1:8,21).

The storm that beset his faith could not deter him from his course, for he had the right set to his soul. Like Isaiah he could say, "I have set my face like a flint, and I know that I shall not be ashamed" (Isa. 50:7); and like the Psalmist who declared, "I have set the Lord always before me...and I shall not be moved" (Psa. 16:8). It was the set of the soul that made the difference. The sails were set before the storm, and kept right during the storm. The storm did not determine Daniel's course, they simply became his servants.

Windswept child of God, it is our responsibility to see that the sails of our soul are rightly set and kept to make sure our vessel holds to the course. We see people who fail to do so, and they suffer shipwreck and loss. Under the strong tempest of disaster one man is driven on the rocks, the other driven into the harbor of God's mercy. It is the way the sails are set that determines the outcome. If our sails are properly rigged, the storm that may sink another's ship, will simply sweep us on to blessing.

> Ships sail east and ships sail west,
> While the selfsame breezes blow;
> It's the set of the sails,
> And not the gales,
> That determine the way they go.

> Like the ships of the sea, are the ways of men;
> As they journey along through life.
> It's the set of the soul,
> That determines the goal,
> And not the calm nor strife.

Ether removed from air allows
fire to burn & not be seen —
utter darkness